MOVEMENT MENTORS

Dred Scott, Homer Plessy, and Rev. Oliver Brown

Three Courageous Men, Their Landmark
Cases, and Their Enduring Legacies

FIRST EDITION

BRIAN K. LEONARD, J.D., LL.M., ESQ.

CIVIL WRITES PRESS

Copyright © 2021 by Brian K. Leonard
All rights reserved.

Library of Congress Cataloging in Publication Data:
Leonard, Brian K.
Movement Mentors: Dred Scott, Homer Plessy, and Rev. Oliver Brown, Three Courageous Men, Three Landmark Cases, and Three Enduring Legacies - 1st ed.

MOVEMENT MENTORS

To my Wife and daughters with whom
I get to share this great opportunity and
a labor of love.
To my readers who I hope will be enriched and
inspired by this work.

ACKNOWLEDGMENTS

THIS BOOK WAS MADE possible by countless people, family, friends, and supporters along the way. To all those who invested in me and it, I hope that this work lives up to all that I believe it can be for others to enjoy. In particular, I would like to thank, my editor, for her assistance with this book.

CONTENTS

Acknowledgments .... *vii*

Introduction *1*

CHAPTER 1: To Ask the Unthinkable: Dred Scott 5

CHAPTER 2: Dred Scott: An Infamous Case 23

CHAPTER 3: The Legacy of Dred Scott 45

CHAPTER 4: The Activist: Homer Plessy 65

CHAPTER 5: A Case of Conscience: Plessy v. Ferguson 85

CHAPTER 6: Fail Up: The Outcomes of Plessy 107

CHAPTER 7: An Education: The Road to Brown 129

CHAPTER 8: Reaching the Mountain Top 147

CHAPTER 9: The Struggle Continues 167

CHAPTER 10: Lessons from Movement Mentors 187

Notes *207*

INTRODUCTION

THROUGHOUT THE HISTORY OF the United States, there have been few cases that have called into question the morality and basic human decency of this country, as the *Dred Scott v. Sandford* (1857), *Plessy v. Ferguson* (1896), and *Brown v. the Board of Education of Topeka Kansas* (1954) cases. These cases pulled on the moral fiber of our country; with the first two almost tearing it asunder, and last one, holding our union together. They arose at the intersection of race, politics and law, and constitute the legal backdrop for the periods of Reconstruction, Jim Crow Segregation, and the Modern Civil Rights Movement of the 1950's and 1960's in this country. At the heart of these landmark cases, were three courageous men with incredible stories: Dred Scott, Homer Plessy, and Rev. Oliver Brown.

Dred Scott's case was about slavery, but it became about more than that. It became, about citizenship and basic civil rights. As it turns out all three men's cases were about citizenship and enjoyment of the full rights thereof. Each man's story and case took place in largely different generations of this country and of African Americans. But it is impossible to tell the story of the journey of African Americans' struggle for civil rights in the U.S. without discussion of these men and their cases figuring prominently. Each had its own constitutional and legal theories and ramifications. However, each had their own impact on society and the lives of African Americans in this country. What's also interesting about the actual cases is that two out of the three men lost their cases at the Supreme Court. Yet even in losing, they gained something. Of course, in the case of Dred Scott, he was after his freedom, which he eventually received. Homer Plessy on the other hand attempted to change his conditions and those of others around him. Like Rev. Oliver Brown, he was aware that his case could potentially change conditions for other African Americans, albeit for public accommodations.

Ultimately, it was Rev. Oliver Brown's case, on behalf of his daughter, Linda, who would help to right the wrong created by Plessy's and Dred's cases. This book is necessary, as whether knowingly or unknowingly, these men were not only part of a movement, but they were also leaders, and serve as mentors for current and future movements. They played a central part in shaping the civil rights history of this country. Although they had many other attributes, these men all had one indelible quality: courage. They brought these cases at times when their lives, their families, and their very existence were threatened. They understood, in the words of a great historian, that the difference between a movement and a moment is sacrifice,[1] they were willing to make the necessary sacrifice. They believed that even in pursuing what most considered to be a lost cause, they could make strides for change. They understood Fredrick Douglas, when he said, "if there is no struggle, there is no progress."[2]

Furthermore, Dr. Martin Luther King, Jr., famously remarked, "...[T]he arc of the moral universe is long, but it bends toward justice."[3] Former President Barack H. Obama, went even further and remarked that, "the moral arc of the universe may bend toward justice, but it does not bend by itself."[4] These three men and their cases helped bend the moral arc of the universe "toward justice," by fighting the struggle for civil rights and social justice in their own time. However, in taking up struggle it is not without costs. The experiences of these three courageous men, created movements, which ushered in a new era for Civil Rights in this country.

Scott, Plessy, and Rev. Brown, and their cases are not just unique and important because of their place in civil rights law, politics, and history. They are also important because their cases force us to turn inward and examine within ourselves what the principles imitated in these cases, like freedom, dignity, and equality, really mean.[5] Although these cases came about in relatively different eras of this country's history, they do share common themes and lessons. Not only is it important to analyze the common themes from these cases, but the three men at the center of these cases should be studied along with the three constitutional provisions involved.

Accordingly, this book is organized in three parts. Part I discusses Dred Scott, Part II, Homer Plessy, and Part III, Rev. Oliver Brown, respectively. The aim of the first chapter of each part is to provide a back story for each case: to show the real people who were at the heart of these cases: to bring the reader into their lives and hopefully give the reader of sense of why these people chose or were chosen to lead these fights. The aim of the second chapter in each part, takes the reader to each of the cases, to illustrate on basic level, the legal background and history of the cases, then the decisions themselves and how they were resolved. The goal here is not to perform a very tight legal analysis but to provide the legal context for the reader to understand and appreciate the gravity with which each case had and continues to have for us today. The last chapter of each part ends by discussing the legacy of each man and their case. The idea here is to help the reader conceptualize the impact of each man and their cases both in their time, and afterwards. The last chapter in the book synthesizes lessons that each man, their case, and their legacy teach current and future generations about movements. The goal is to conclude with enduring lessons from each man's journey, that can be applicable to the struggle for civil and human rights today and beyond. Now to introduce to you the reader the Movement Mentors: Dred Scott, Homer Plessy, and Rev. Oliver Brown.

CHAPTER 1

TO ASK THE UNTHINKABLE: *DRED SCOTT*

THIS IS THE STORY of a journey that began in the cradle of US slavery, the Commonwealth of Virginia.[1] His journey would take him all the way to the US Supreme Court. But first there would be stops in Alabama, Louisiana, the mighty Mississippi River, and later, Missouri. This is a story of an American family—probably not the typical American family, but the typical African American family of late eighteenth- and early nineteenth-century America. It is a story about a simple family whose patriarch had a simple name: Dred Scott.

It may be difficult to trace his exact roots, as, like many enslaved persons, Scott was not included in the census, nor are there any birth records to determine exactly when he was born. It is somewhat prophetic that he was most likely born in Virginia, where enslaved persons were first brought to the American colonies in 1619. Around the time of the beginning of the American Revolution, the number of slaves almost equaled the number of whites living in Virginia;[2] in Scott's time, it had more slaves than any other state; and in some counties, particularly in the southeastern part of the state, there were more enslaved people than whites.[3] Indeed, enslaved persons made up almost 30 percent of Virginia's population overall.[4] It was a large state and one of the most prominent in the tobacco trade during Scott's time.[5] Although this was where he started out, over the course of his life he would travel, much like his case, to many different states.

Peter Blow lived on his plantation in Southampton County, Virginia, not far from the Virginia–North Carolina border. Based on piecemeal records, Scott was among the enslaved persons he owned and brought with him when he moved to Alabama in 1818.[6] Researchers have been able to determine that Scott's mother was living in Southampton County, Virginia as an enslaved person on the 860-acre Blow Plantation at the time he was born.[7]

Dred Scott- Courtesy of the Missouri Historical Society

For almost his entire life, Scott lived as an enslaved person. He would be taken from, and across, at least six states. He would marry (or have a civil union) and have a family. But he would remain enslaved. His freedom would be a dream deferred. It appears that he was referred to as Sam growing up owned by the Blow family, but he later changed his name to Dred. By choosing his name, he was attempting to create his own identity rather than continue to be labeled with the identity put upon him by the slaveholders who owned him. Naming was important back then, not only in terms of keeping records; in many instances, but the forced changing of an enslaved person's name was also a means of disconnecting them from their identity, and especially from their history, origin, and ancestors in Africa. This was essential to the continued enslavement of the African people. Perhaps as a sign of things to come, Dred attempted to claim some semblance of his culture or identity in choosing his name. It is not clear where he got this name or why he chose it, but it was his, and he was able to develop some measure of strength and courage from the fact that he chose his own name, something that had been denied to many enslaved people. His struggle for identity, dignity, and freedom would become a wonderful chapter in the American story.

Dred Scott is ultimately most famous for the case that bears his name, in which he sought his freedom and which he brought at a time of great turmoil and great challenge in a country whose dominant culture did not even consider him to be a person. While some states had begun to prohibit slavery within their territorial borders, such as Pennsylvania as early as 1789, this was not the tenor of most of the young country. By the time of Dred Scott, the nation had not even celebrated its centennial. Indeed, the peculiar institution of slavery was far older than the budding country, but the nation had yet to come to terms with it. It is here upon this backdrop that we find Dred Scott.

While many historians would disagree on this point, it can be argued that Scott's case became a catalyst to the prosecution of the Civil War, the abolition of slavery, and, ultimately, the recognition of formerly enslaved persons as citizens of the United States. Many of the rights that were made legally available as a result of Dred Scott's case and example were not fully enjoyed until the next century—the time of the next two men discussed in this book.

On the legal side, the *Dred Scott* case began as two cases. Both Dred and his wife Harriett filed lawsuits in 1846 challenging their enslaved condition, since they both had been taken to and resided in states or territories where slavery had been outlawed. That Harriett Scott had her own claim to freedom is a subtle but important point in Dred Scott's story. Like Dred, Harriett was also likely born in Virginia, but she was taken to Fort Snelling and lived there two to three years prior to Dred, as an enslaved person of Major Lawrence Taliafero.[8] It was commonplace for officers to bring slaves into the Louisiana Territory, which included Fort Snelling. This despite the Missouri Compromise's prohibition of slavery in the territory.

The Scotts' Life

Scott was no stranger to moving around, similar to many enslaved persons of that time—or of any time, for that matter—but one move would prove momentous: in 1830 he was taken to the state for which he would become famous and his case would become infamous: Missouri—specifically, St. Louis, where he was eventually sold to Dr. John Emerson before the end of 1833.[9] After about a year, Dr. Emerson and Scott traveled to Fort Armstrong, in the free state of Illinois, based on orders from the Army for Dr. Emerson.[10] Almost three years later, after closure of Fort Armstrong, Dr. Emerson was once again transferred to Fort Snelling in the Iowa territory, in the current state of Minnesota.[11] There Scott met the future Mrs. Harriett Scott, also an enslaved person. They were married through what was considered a formal civil union on September 14, 1837, by the justice of the peace, Major Taliafero, who also sold Harriett to Emerson. (The Scotts' union could not have been considered a marriage, as by law Negroes were not permitted to marry at that time.)[12] As was customary, Dr. Emerson hired the Scotts out while at Fort Snelling, and eventually left them there under the control of others to whom he hired the Scotts out in 1837.[13] After getting married himself, to Eliza Irene Sanford the next year, and after being ordered to Florida, Dr. Emerson once again left the Scotts in the custody of those to whom he hired them out, this time for good in 1840.[14]

From a legal perspective, Scott's journey to the Supreme Court started when he accompanied Emerson on the doctor's December 1833 enlistment in the Army, an experiment with military service at Fort Armstrong and Rock Island, Illinois, in the Mississippi River.[15] Later, in May 1836, Scott accompanied Emerson when he was transferred to Fort Snelling in Wisconsin. This is significant, as Wisconsin was acquired in the Louisiana Purchase, and slavery was outlawed in the Louisiana Territory by the Missouri Compromise.[16] This, coupled with the fact that Scott was owned by Emerson in not one but two free states, further buttressed Scott's claim of freedom.[17] Ultimately, the fact that the Scotts were taken to these areas where slavery was not allowed would prove very important in their story.

Given the fact that he was allowed to form a civil union, there are a few understandings we can glean about Scott at this time in his history. First, he was ambitious, as he pursued his own legitimacy in marrying and having a family. In addition, it is likely that he was respected in many ways, as he was taken to several different states, and his wife's purchase by Emerson evidences the importance that Emerson placed on him. His way of being must have been such that people were willing to help him. These included the attorneys who would prove willing to take his case, friends, and a minister willing to step in and compensate for his inability to read or write. Even the Blow family, who originally held young Scott and his family as enslaved persons, provided financial support for him and his cause as well as eventually granted him his freedom once he lost his case at the US Supreme Court. All these folks being willing to get behind him suggest a person who was seen as worth sacrificing for and providing for. Moreover, his cause was a noble one, as it is reported that despite what the country and other enslaved persons might have believed he was doing,[18] Scott did not have political aspirations, necessarily, but was simply seeking the freedom that had been denied him.

Eventually, Dred and Harriett started a family. They had four children; two of them did not survive infancy.[19] Like their parents, the Scotts' children were born as enslaved persons, and the Scotts would eventually attempt to change that condition. It is entirely possible that one of Dred Scott's motives for bringing his famous lawsuit was that he did not want his family to remain enslaved, especially his children. Long before Dr. Martin Luther King Jr. talked about his dream, Dred had a dream. He dreamed that he, his wife and his children would one day be free. In fact, prior to bringing the lawsuit, he attempted to purchase his family's freedom as well as his own. Unfortunately, his first attempt was not successful.

Life for Dred and Harriett was likely similar to that of many enslaved persons at that time. It is not clear what Dred's profession was, but it is believed that he was more likely than not a slave who worked in the house, as he did not appear to have the physical attributes that would have been useful in the fields. Dred did not appear to be a tall or muscular man. Instead, he was likely better suited physically for domestic and/or janitorial work. There is some indication that he may have served as a janitor, which gives us an indication of the types of duties he would have performed as an enslaved person. This could include duties that later would be performed by a butler in a more civilized society, one that did not engage in such an abhorrent practice as the institution of American chattel slavery. It is likely that someone in his family or someone who was also enslaved by the Blow family in Alabama taught him their line of work or allowed him to apprentice, as he had learned his trades sufficiently to be useful to Emerson. Given the conditions of his era, he most likely did not live in the house with the slave/plantation owners but was instead relegated to slave quarters, as were many enslaved persons at that time. He likely had quarters with Harriett, his wife, who would attempt to make their quarters as much of a home as she possibly could under the circumstances. Given his longevity in his circumstances, it is likely that whatever work Dred performed, he was good at it. Indeed, later on, he would become a hotel porter and Harriett would become a laundress.

It is not clear what Harriett's duties were, but given the circumstances, it is likely that she performed household duties for their masters, possibly including cooking, cleaning, and caring for the masters' children. In addition, it is apparent that Dred and Harriett were both loaned out by those that enslaved them, on a number of occasions. At the same time, they had to deal with the problems of marriage under a slaveholding regime. Attempting to raise a family under those conditions or even to keep their family together was very difficult. Their two children had to be cared for and provided for, to the extent possible.

As is the case with many enslaved people in history, very little is known about Scott's past or his family due to scant information, including lack of birth certificates or other records, beyond property records. It is not clear whether Scott's parents were as courageous as he, or where he received his mettle. But he pressed forward toward freedom with the knowledge that he came from a proud people. It is not clear if Scott knew what part of Africa he was from or what tribe his ancestors belonged to. He was born in the new country, the United States of America, not in Africa; and in this country he was regarded as merely three-fifths of a person, or as property. He came to believe that he could be free, that he had some of the same rights as those who enslaved him. Having lived in both slave states and free states, possibly it was the glimpse of freedom with his own eyes that gave him hope that he could be free one day.

So here we have Dred and Harriett, enslaved persons all their lives up to this point, with the courage and conviction to believe that they deserved their freedom. What great reserves of strength and courage Mr. and Mrs. Scott had developed during such a time.

Dred and Harriett Scott as Movement Mentors

The Scotts are heroes of the highest order. Their lives weave together a beautiful liberation narrative that has spanned generations and that will continue to be told in generations to come. There are many lessons that new generations of movement leaders and activists can learn from Dred and Harriett Scott. Likely very proud people, as they would demonstrate through their activism, they stand as early movement mentors for all generations. Dred Scott rose up at a time when it was not only unpopular, it was largely unthinkable for a slave to use the court system to seek his rights, in the manner in which he did. Even in defeat, Dred Scott teaches future movement leaders about the necessity of seeking justice for oneself and for one's family. The Scotts believed that they were entitled to basic human rights, such as the right to marry, the right to raise their children, and the right to their freedom to go and be whatever they chose. Not only did they believe these things, they had the courage to act on them. They were early civil rights activists, embodying the ideal that even if you lose the fight, the fact that you fought at all still brings the issue forward. Despite the fact that they lost their cases in the court system, they won their cases in the court of public opinion. So much so that after the Supreme Court's decision, the relatives of Peter Blow eventually granted them their freedom.[20]

Another important observation about the Scotts is the revelation that education alone is not a predictor of one's activism. Of the three men discussed in this book, Dred Scott was probably the least educated, literate, and sophisticated; however, his story may be more powerful given the context in which it occurred. Most likely, Dred and Harriett could not read or write—first, because it was forbidden by law; second, because they did not have a basic education. In fact, as will be discussed below, Dred could only sign an X for his name on any legal pleadings. Still, he was able to convince lawyers to support and represent him in his eventual fight for his freedom.

Moreover, he possessed the courage it took even to conceive that, in the same country in which he was enslaved, he could be set free. Without Dred Scott, there would be no Homer Plessy, nor would there be a Rev. Oliver Brown. What was it about Scott that made him believe that the fight was worth the struggle, that he could take his case to court, and that he could eventually win? He did not let the wall of obstacles in front of him deter his efforts. While it is true that he had a lot of help along the way, as will be discussed below, he still had to be the one to stand up.

Scott's fight for his freedom became a microcosm of what was happening across the country. In essence, by seeking his freedom, Scott began his own Civil Rights movement. Like many African Americans, Scott represented the entire race, beyond his and his wife's own individual cases. As his case went, so would the mood of African Americans across the country. Like many movements, Scott's struggle began as a simple journey toward his own self-exploration and actualization. He was proof that African Americans were more than enslaved persons, more than property. He stood as a shining beacon of hope to other African Americans. His life was evidence that enslaved persons of African descent were more complex and intelligent than slave owners and whites generally thought. Less than three hundred years after his forebears were brought to the United States, Scott asked the country to define freedom for enslaved persons. In a country where many presidents, members of Congress, and yes, even judges including Justices of the Supreme Court, themselves owned enslaved persons, Scott had the sense of spirit and drive to pursue this ideal, to ask the unthinkable, to seek the unreachable, to dream the impossible dream. Although things were beginning to change across the country, the idea of moving away from slavery would, like many paradigm shifts, take time, effort, and yes, even war. But Scott was before all of this.

Scott was a visionary. His devotion to his family, to his children, can been seen throughout his life and throughout the fight for his freedom. Scott symbolizes Benjamin Disraeli's expressed belief: "nothing can resist a human will that will stake its very existence on its purpose."[21] Dred and Harriett's cause was one that sparked a movement, a precursor to Reconstruction.

Also fascinating about Scott's case is what it represents. Although the historical record is clear that he was not the first individual to file a lawsuit seeking freedom,[22] his case became the most famous and the most infamous at the same time. As will be discussed in more detail in chapter 2, Scott's case was unique in that, as much as it was about individual freedom for himself and his family, it also attacked the very heart of the institution of slavery. While we know that he ultimately desired freedom for himself and his family, what we do not know is where this drive for freedom came from. Did this drive for freedom come from his African ancestors? His parents were owned by the Blow family in Virginia, and so it is likely that given his age he was at least three generations removed from the first enslaved persons brought to America.

It is worth noting that, with the challenges we have today, nothing we have faced or are facing compares to what was behind and ahead for Dred and Harriett Scott. Prior to being freed, eventually, through the action of the Blow family, neither Dred nor Harriett knew of any existence where slavery was not a reality. Even when they traveled to states that had been designated free by virtue of the Missouri Compromise, it was as though Dred and Harriett could only be spectators to freedom, prior to their forced return to the slave states from which they had departed. One wonders, what did they talk about? Did they dream of securing their freedom one day? Did they fantasize about what it would be like to be free, finally? Did they envision their grandchildren being free, or their descendants? When was the decision made to seek their freedom?

As noted earlier, Harriett filed her own action seeking freedom as well. Did they discuss this together and come up with a joint decision to fight for their freedom? Why did they seek a more civilized pursuit of their freedom? They did not choose the route of Nat Turner, nor that of Frederick Douglass. Dred was likely somewhere in the middle between these two men who sought freedom for their people in their own ways. Like their names, the name Dred Scott would become synonymous with the struggle for African American freedom and, eventually, equality.

Dred and Harriett were already barrier breakers by virtue of their civil union. Their desire to have and raise a family also put them in an unusual place. Thus, it was likely not a stretch that they would seek to reach beyond even the limits that they had already tested in search of the ultimate prize, their freedom. The Scotts embody perseverance, resistance, persistence, and all the qualities that can be ascribed to two people who were unwilling to give up. They carried their fight all the way to the end. As in their day-to-day life, it is likely that they had their share of aches and pains to deal with as they proceeded with their case: pressures from people and circumstances as well as all the difficulties attendant to any endeavor of an enslaved person. But through it all, they stayed the course.

It is not clear whether Dred and Harriett were religious followers. Even enslaved persons were permitted to take part in some type of religious ceremony led by another enslaved person or the slaveholder. Despite the obvious contradiction, many slaveholders aligned themselves with religion and the pursuit of God though they had no problem with slavery. Some scholars have theorized that such double mindedness was made possible by or at least was attributable to biblical verses instructing slaves to obey their masters. If Dred and Harriett were religious believers, it is likely that their faith helped to sustain them and hold them up. If they were followers of the Judeo-Christian tradition, they likely relied on the teachings of the Old Testament struggle of the children of Israel to be freed from the hands of the Egyptian Pharaoh.

By the time Dred and Harriett sought their freedom, their labor of enslaved persons was a key commodity to the Southern states. Slavery's enormous value went beyond the cotton industry; indeed, enslaved persons were utilized in just about every major industry in the South. It was thought at that time that slavery was the South's advantage and the factor many in the South felt helped to level the economic playing field with the North.

Quite possibly, Dred and Harriet picked the best and the worst time to challenge slavery and sue for their freedom. The worst time, perhaps, as slavery had become as widespread and entrenched in the budding country as any other institution; and despite the demarcation of slave states and free states, it was clear that to end slavery at that time would create havoc throughout the South, and the North as well, at least on a national level. Despite these factors, Dred and Harriett continued through the struggle and the pain to press forward to their goal.

At the same time, Dred and Harriett's challenge came at the best of times. The issue of slavery was beginning to come to a boiling point for the country. It would either be embraced nationally and spread throughout the West, or it would end. Both results were not possible. In the North, there arose calls for slavery's end, while there were calls in the South not only for its survival but for its thriving. Something had to give.

The Why

It is likely that Dred and Harriett were aware that they would be in for a fight and that it was one they would almost certainly lose. Eventually, Dred's freedom would be secured outside of the courts, which begs the question of whether their cases were necessary. It is in the answer to this question that current and future generations of Americans can take heed.

Regardless of their individual motives for legal action, the goal of their fight became bigger than their individual freedom. Here, their African roots of community and village may have been at play. If Dred, and consequently Harriett, were able to secure their individual freedom, the attention garnered by their cases, could assist other African Americans who might be able to use the outcome to gain their own freedom.

The byproduct of this attention was greater awareness by those in the North about the horrors and wrongs of slavery. Immediately before the Scotts' cases arose, there were at least a half million enslaved people throughout the South, working in cotton mills, steel mills, salt mines, lead mines, on river boats, as blacksmiths, and in many other functions of the economy and society.[23] These enslaved people performed many essential services, yet they were denied the most basic and essential rights of human beings. Perhaps waging even, a losing case would force the South to show its hand: its deep ties to slavery and unwillingness to part with it.

At the same time, the Scotts would force the North to make a decision, either to fight to end slavery or to acknowledge their participation in it, whether unwilling or not. Either way, something had to be done, and the Scotts may have been keenly aware of this fact. Their cases, shining the spotlight on slavery once and for all, would force a reckoning. They knew that their cause was just, and they found the courage to pursue it. It is unlikely that either of them believed their case would plunge the country into a civil war, but they realized that creating change would require sacrifice for themselves and others. Their cases became a flagship for each enslaved person, brought on behalf of all those who might not have had the ability, will, or circumstances to bring such a legal challenge. Dred and Harriett would assume the burden and be the ones bringing the challenge.

The scene was set: here we have a climactic battle over slavery before the civil war that was yet to be fought over it. But this battle was not fought with guns or on a battlefield. It was fought in courts of law and public opinion, with pride and dignity, self-respect, and respect for this nation as one that is governed by laws and not men. This does not suggest that those who fight in wars do not do so with dignity and respect for their own beliefs. It merely draws the distinction that the Scotts path was different. This battle was brought by neither heads of state nor by soldiers in uniform. This battle was brought not by congressmen or senators, but by two people—a husband and father, a wife and mother—who dreamed of what this nation could be, should be, and wanted to make it so; who attempted to get this nation to rise up and live out the true meaning of its creed: "we hold these truths to be self-evident, that all men are created equal."[24]

We now know that Dred and Harriett Scott were ahead of their time by leaps and bounds. But what is greatness, if not reaching beyond what is currently present to stretch to what can be. To go where there is no path and leave a trail. To create the circumstances sought and to chart one's own course and carve out one's own mountain. That is what the Scotts represent: greatness in their own time and in ours.

It is likely that Dred Scott never knew of or thought about what his legacy would be. Nevertheless, he left an indelible mark on American life and certainly American legal jurisprudence. It is very likely that the election of Abraham Lincoln, the Civil War, and ultimately Reconstruction are all parts of the legacy of this unassuming man of average stature, whose courage caused him to stand tallest among men of his time. He and his wife Harriett, even some 160 years after their cases were decided, are still speaking and having an impact today. Given what is known about Scott's motives for seeking his freedom, it is unlikely that he wished for such a legacy, and he most certainly did not plan for it. Was it coincidence, or a perfect storm that came together for him to seek his freedom? Dred and Harriett were ordinary people who happened to accomplish the extraordinary. They represent the best of what we can become as a nation and as a people. Whether through slavery, Reconstruction, or the Civil Rights Movement, at varying points in our nation's history, African Americans have been the pulse of

America. In the same way, Dred Scott's life and his case served as the conscience of the nation.

It is clear from Chief Justice Taney's opinion that since being brought to the colonies from Africa, the federal government has not known what to do with the African people.[25] This may explain the result in the Scotts' cases. But it also explains their pursuit of freedom. There must have been some inspiration, some restlessness, something on a very basic and personal level that drove Dred Scott to keep going, to believe that he was right and that despite legal technicalities to the contrary, his family was entitled to be free. They were human beings like any white person, and there was no reasonable basis to deny them their freedom.

Dred and Harriett also represented the impact that one man, one family, one couple with a dream and the perseverance to see their dream come true, could accomplish. Their desire to be free rang throughout the nation. While their minister and friends helped with encouragement, the Blow family with finances, and their attorneys with the legal arguments, it was Dred Scott's name on the case and his family's freedom on the line. At great risk, he fought all the way to highest court in the land for their freedom. Their friends surely had to be inspired by them, as were other enslaved people. It is likely that Dred and Harriett shared their fears and apprehensions with each other and with their friends. They must have felt many different emotions, from dread, to fear, to joy, to anxiety. Nevertheless, they pressed forward. One wonders if they ever thought about giving up their fight and accepting their reality as it was. Did Dred get tired and want to give up, only to be encouraged by Harriett? And in the same way, did Harriett want to give up or, even more, want Dred to give up his fight, due to the toll it would take on their family and their livelihood? As with any movement, there were likely detractors. The family could have been ostracized or vilified even by other enslaved persons for having the temerity to fight for their freedom. There were likely whispers about whether they deserved their freedom, or what was so special about Dred and Harriett that they would think they should succeed where others had failed. They likely faced dissention and betrayal in their own ranks, from the time of filing the case until its conclusion and afterward.

Dred's case spanned at least eleven years, from the time of its filing at the state level, to its completion at the U.S. Supreme Court. This was an incredible amount of time for them to endure, with the legal status of their very lives in jeopardy. And in defeat, there surely could have been times when either of them felt embarrassed about the ultimate loss, or even questioned whether the fight had been for naught, particularly given the great costs to them and their family personally. But it is likely that Scott was not regretful. He may have been disappointed with the Supreme Court's ultimate decision, but not with the fight. It is unlikely that anything in his legal case could come close to comparing to what the family had to endure during their lives as enslaved persons.

Dred Scott began one of the greatest campaigns in the fight for human dignity and equality for African Americans in this country. As a movement mentor, Dred, and his wife Harriett, proved that they had what it took to fight in their time and to pave the way for others to fight, and eventually to win in many instances. His struggle for equality and justice continues to this day and will be won, if the people doing the fighting are as committed and courageous as Dred Scott.

CHAPTER 2

DRED SCOTT: AN INFAMOUS CASE

MOST SCHOLARS, LAWYERS, LEGAL historians, and even judges freely acknowledge that in the US Supreme Court's more than 230-year history, the *Dred Scott v. Sandford* case is likely the most challenging to explain. While it is true that the case was decided in a markedly different time for the United States, politically, socially, and culturally, it is most likely the case about which the Court feels most embarrassed, particularly today. There is enough animosity toward the decision to render it one of the most regrettable blights on the Supreme Court. Not only do many scholars believe it was wrongly decided, but the case also issued a nationwide call to cement slavery's place in American society.

For much of its early existence, the Supreme Court had not been particularly active. That is, until *Marbury v. Madison* was decided in 1803, establishing the concept of judicial review by federal courts of legislative or executive action.[1] Once this was done, the Court took on a new role: arbiter of the Constitution. However, a populist election, leading to the rise of Andrew Jackson to the presidency in

1829 and his subsequent appointments to the Supreme Court, ushered in a new era of Jacksonian jurisprudence. The *Dred Scott* case would later become the hallmark of this time in the Court's history.

By 1856, the Supreme Court was made up of several Justices from the South, which greatly depended upon slavery for its economic survival and its entire societal system. Thus, bringing a case such as this one before this Supreme Court had an almost certain result. But the decision in *Dred Scott* is only part of the story. There are several important principles involved in the beginning and middle of the case that illuminate how the Court ultimately reached its infamous decision.

Dred Scott v. Sandford is really a tale of two cases. Dred and Harriett Scott both filed lawsuits, *Dred Scott v. Emerson* and *Harriett Scott v. Emerson*, on April 6, 1846, in Missouri State Circuit Court.[2] The initial lawyer for the Scotts was Francis B. Murdoch, although later, over the next couple of years, the Scotts would work with several lawyers.[3] These lawyers were Charles D. Drake, Samuel Mansfield Bay, Alex P. Field, and later, David N. Hall.[4] The parties acknowledged that in the midst of the case, the Scotts had been sold to Sanford, and thus the case was renamed to replace Emerson with Sanford, the name with which this case would be recorded in history. The parties offered no additional evidence or witnesses beyond the evidence that the Scotts had been taken to, and lived with Emerson in, non-slave states.

During this time, slavery had become the rule rather than the exception. The "peculiar institution" was legal in fifteen states and by its operation divided the country geographically. By the time the Scotts filed their lawsuit, they were in Missouri, and they filed their cases in Missouri state court, known then as the Circuit Court of St. Louis. Their lawsuit was filed against Emerson's widow, to whom the Scotts had been passed upon his death. Apparently, Mrs.

Emerson hired out the Scotts regularly or for extended periods of time. It is likely that, in addition to seeking their freedom, the Scotts preferred not to be hired out to work for other whites any further.

In filing their lawsuit, the Scotts were aided by the Blow family, who formerly owned Scott, and Minister John R. Anderson of the Second African Baptist Church, who had experience helping enslaved people like the Scotts seek their freedom. As indicated in chapter 1, this assistance was crucial given Scott's inability to read or write at the time. Utilizing Anderson's assistance, and with the financial assistance of the Blow family, the Scotts were able to contact the lawyer Francis B. Murdoch, who filed their petitions in court.

To understand the legal background to their petitions, it is important to understand the state of the law on slavery at the time. Virginia, the state where the Scotts most likely were born, began formally allowing slavery in 1661.[5] Virginia continued to enact laws governing slavery, such that by the time Dred was born (circa 1799), it had an elaborate slavery "code" that circumscribed the conduct of enslaved persons in great detail.[6] Following the American Revolutionary War and independence from Great Britain, with the creation of the US Constitution slavery was at least implicitly cemented in the United States. This is seen through the adoption of the three-fifths clause, counting an enslaved person as equivalent to three-fifths of a white person for the purpose of apportionment and representation in Congress.[7] The addition of the clause prohibiting Congress from outlawing slavery prior to 1808 as well as the fugitive slave clause, requiring enslaved persons who escaped to be returned to the slaveholder,[8] rounded out the federal constitutional infrastructure for slavery. Thus, at least insofar as the original U.S. Constitution was concerned, in the absence of Congressional action, it was largely left to the individual states to decide the question of slavery.

One such decision was enacted with the Northwest Ordinance, adopted in 1787 and amended in 1789, which created the Northwest Territory, governing the expansion of the United States. Importantly, the Northwest Ordinance, prohibited slavery within the territories north of the Ohio River.

At the same time, slavery proliferated throughout the South.[9] In fact, as the United States began to expand and more states were added to the Union, there was growing concern about the number of slave states, where slavery was still permitted, and free states, where slavery was prohibited in some form. It is an interesting dichotomy, as slavery was a major issue as the Union was formed, and its inclusion would eventually threaten to tear the Union apart.

This chorus of controversy swelled to a level at which Congress was forced to act. The result was the Missouri Compromise of 1820, prohibiting slavery north of the 36°30 parallel.[10] Despite the act's name, Missouri was excluded from this prohibition, making it a slave state. But this proved insufficient, and Congress enacted another measure, the Compromise of 1850.[11] In this act, Congress agreed that California would enter the United States as a free state while other territories in the west would be created without mentioning slavery; slaveholders would receive greater protection with a stronger fugitive slave law; and slavery would not be allowed in the District of Columbia.[12] Finally, hoping the third time would be the charm, Congress passed the Kansas-Nebraska Act of 1854. This act provided that Kansas and Nebraska would be territories, and their legislatures would decide whether slavery would be allowed within their boundaries.[13]

A few years earlier, though, in 1842, the US Supreme Court decided in *Prigg v. Pennsylvania*—a case that likely could have benefited the Scotts—that state officials in the free state of Pennsylvania were not required to assist in returning an enslaved person to a slaveholder from Maryland, a slave state.[14]

Although the Scotts were currently residing in Missouri, a slave state, at the time their case was filed in court, they previously lived in territories that were considered free. These included Illinois and the northern section of the Louisiana Territory.[15] Ultimately, prior to filing his case, Dred lived in free territories for a total of almost seven years.[16] The Scotts' petitions were based on the argument that enslaved people who lived in a free state could seek to obtain their freedom on that basis, and therefore, under the Northwest Ordinance and the Missouri Compromise, they were entitled to their freedom from slavery. While it was settled law in Missouri courts, that a master was entitled to travel to free states and territories with an enslaved person without losing their right of ownership, Missouri courts also held that when a formerly enslaved person took residence in a free state, even for a short period, their enslavement does not re-attach if they return to Missouri.[17]

The Scotts' lawyer, Samuel M. Bay, attempted to offer testimony at trial that Dred Scott was enslaved by Mrs. Emerson in Missouri and accompanied her to Fort Armstrong and Fort Snelling.[18] George W. Goode was the original lawyer for Emerson, but he was eventually replaced by Hugh A. Garland, who argued that Bay had not proven that Mrs. Emerson claimed Dred Scott as a slave. However, Samuel Russell, the Scotts' would-be star witness, admitted that he did not have first-hand knowledge of their condition of enslavement.[19]

As a result, without additional evidence, unsurprisingly and fairly quickly, on November 19, 1846, the jury returned a verdict in favor of Emerson and against the Scotts.[20] Meanwhile, Bay filed a motion for a new trial on July 1, 1847, and a new trial was granted for December 2 of that same year.[21] In the new trial, the Scotts were victorious. The jury returned a verdict in their favor. The defendant,

Mrs. Emerson responded by appealing to the Missouri Supreme Court. On March 22, 1852, that court remanded the case back to the trial court, citing two cases: *The Slave Grace* and *Strader v. Graham*.[22] In *The Slave Grace*, the High Court of Admiralty ruled that Grace, an enslaved woman, did not obtain her freedom merely by traveling to England in 1822, which had abolished slavery by that time. In addition, in *Strader v. Graham*, the US Supreme Court recognized the Northwest Ordinance's control of the territories governed by it at its inception but did not extend its application to states subsequently added to the United States.[23] In *Strader*, three enslaved persons fled from Kentucky, first to Indiana, then to Ohio, and later to Canada. The Court in *Strader* held that the law of the state from which the enslaved persons traveled, Kentucky—not the state to which they traveled, Ohio—determined their status as enslaved persons or free persons.[24] In sending the case back to the trial court, the Missouri Supreme Court, analogized these two cases to the Scotts' cases, ultimately deciding that despite the Scotts' travel to free states, their status did not change, but would be determined by the laws of Missouri, a slave state.

Notwithstanding this result on or about November 2, 1853, while the cases were still pending in state court, the Scotts' new attorney, Roswell M. Field, filed a separate action in the US Circuit Court.[25] This filing would eventually take the Scotts' cases, and consequently Dred Scott, into infamy in the annals of US and Constitutional legal history. John F.A. Sanford (the brother-in-law of Dr. Emerson), to whom title to the Scotts were purportedly transferred, was actually listed as the defendant by the Scotts—strategically, as he was a citizen and resident of New York, which they hoped would create diversity jurisdiction in federal court, the significance of which is discussed below.[26] It is this case, *Dred Scott v. Sandford,* (spelled incorrectly) that would eventually become the landmark decision, which would arguably set off a chain reaction throughout the country resulting in the start of the US Civil War; and this reaction would largely continue through the end of that war and on to ratification of the Thirteenth Amendment in 1865, constitutionally abolishing chattel slavery in the United States.

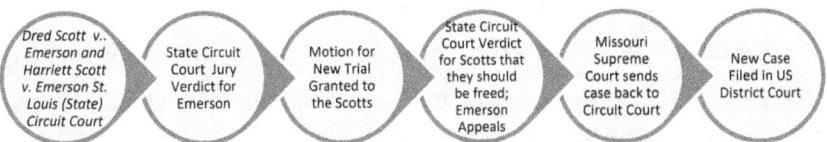

Illustration of the Dred Scott's Case traveling through the Courts

The Scotts lost their case at the US Circuit level, and with the denial of their motion for a new trial, they filed an appeal on December 30, 1854.[27] The case was not heard by the US Supreme Court until 1856. By this time, the lawyers on the two sides of the case were Reverdy Johnson and Henry S. Geyer for Sanford, and Montgomery Blair for the Scotts.[28] Initially, and until re-argument, there was only one brief filed in the case, by Blair, basically focusing on the Scotts' residency in Illinois. The initial arguments took place between February 11 and Valentine's Day, 1856. At the time of the arguments, the case had not yet come to great national attention, save some sporadic coverage.

For example, Horace Greely at the *New York Daily Tribune*, ran an article on February 15 discussing the *Dred Scott* case that was before the Supreme Court.[29] In May the case was ordered for re-argument later that year, with a list of issues for the parties to address. The primary issue was whether the Scotts could be considered citizens for the purpose of diversity jurisdiction. Diversity jurisdiction gives the federal courts the power to hear and decide a case and requires that the case involve citizens of different states on the two sides. The significance of this issue to the case at re-argument had to do with the fact that if Dred Scott was not a citizen, due to his status as an enslaved person, then he would not be able to sue in federal courts, and therefore, theoretically, his case would be dismissed.

At the time of re-argument, Sanford's attorney, Geyer, did file a written brief, and the oral arguments took place in December 1856, some two years after the Scotts initially filed their appeal.

One of the very interesting legal and historical questions regarding the *Dred Scott* decision is whether its majority opinion, issued by Chief Justice Roger B. Taney, was legally necessary—a legal concept known as *obiter dictum*. This issue arises primarily because the bulk of the Court's decision dealt with the legal and historical basis of slavery rather than with the primary legal question. Then, on March 6, 1857, the Court concluded, by a vote of 7-2, that as an enslaved person of African descent, neither Dred Scott nor Harriett Scott were citizens of the state of Missouri or the United States. Therefore, under the rules of diversity jurisdiction, neither the federal courts nor the US Supreme Court had jurisdiction, or the power to hear and decide the Scotts' case.[30]

What makes the majority opinion so intriguing is that an argument can be made that any further discussion or findings beyond this holding, which was a large portion of the opinion in the case, would not become precedent, and therefore other courts would not be required to follow it; so why did Chief Justice Taney bother to write the opinion? What is clear from the opinion is that he was trying to settle the slavery question once and for all.

As stated by the Chief Justice, the central question for the Court concerned the legal status of the descendants of Africans or Negroes who were brought to this country as enslaved persons, whether born to enslaved parents or to free parents: were they citizens within the meaning of the laws of the United States? He took great pains at the beginning of the opinion to examine the history of the United

States and the Constitution to support the contention that Africans or Negroes—whether enslaved or not—were not, nor were they ever intended to be, citizens or even human beings. Instead, his opinion concludes that the only legal status for Africans or Negroes was as property, insofar as federal law was concerned. In fact, Chief Justice Taney argued, infamously, that enslaved persons, Africans, or Negroes had no legal rights that whites were bound by the law to respect. This goes far beyond merely holding that Dred and Harriett were not citizens of the United States.

Chief Justice Taney's opinion seems to suggest a powerful question of the time, and in truth it remains a powerful question for today: What should be done with African Americans? What is their place in this country? Although the ancestors of African Americans were first brought here in 1619, that question remains. More specific to the case, it appears from his opinion, that at least on some level the Chief Justice attempted to give the impression that he wrestled with the status of African Americans. Instead, his opinion made clear in its holding that African Americans were merely property, a decision that would linger for years and would ultimately require a war to resolve. But he was adamant in his holding, and it is clear from his opinion that he perceived the Congress and the president as having failed to fully and adequately address the slavery question.

Chief Justice Roger B. Taney Courtesy of Library of Congress

It is interesting to note that Chief Justice Taney distinguished Native American people from African American people, particularly in regard to their status as a people to be dealt with under the laws of the United States. He concluded that, unlike Native American people, Negroes were always considered to be an inferior race, to be property, and to possess only those powers given to them by the federal government.

The alleged basis for Chief Justice Taney's conclusion was that at the time of the Constitution's adoption some eighty years before, African Americans were not considered citizens, but an inferior race unsuited for relating to whites or socializing with them. He went on to say that this was the case, for more than a century prior to the Constitution's adoption. In addition, he maintained that African

Americans had been considered enslaved persons even back in Great Britain as well as in the thirteen original colonies which later declared independence and adopted the Constitution.

Chief Justice Taney then cited various colonial-era laws that made reference to the African race; and later he cited two clauses in the Constitution that mentioned enslaved people, both discussed above: the provision regarding importing enslaved persons and the provision regarding return of enslaved people to the slaveholders who laid claim to them. He cites these two clauses as proof that the African race and their descendants were always excluded from the promises of the Constitution, including freedom and liberty. Chief Justice Taney is careful to point out that the laws of several slave states support this contention and that even in free states, where slavery had been outlawed, there were restrictive laws such as those against formerly enslaved people marrying whites.

It is important to note some inconsistencies in the Chief Justice's opinion. First, he based his reasoning on some conclusory assumptions. In one such instance, he draws no distinction between Africans who were born free and those who were not. In fact, it appears that the Chief Justice almost entirely avoids this distinction, instead summarily asserting that "Africans" (all Africans, in the absence of any qualifier to the contrary) should be treated a certain way. This logic appears at best superfluous. This is important because had he recognized a distinction; it is unlikely that his opinion could have been phrased in such sweeping terms. It is likely that had he pointed out a difference, it would have detracted from his rendering of the majority opinion in line with his intentions.

Another logical flaw can be pointed out is his argument that Dred Scott, his wife Harriett, and their daughters should not be treated as citizens because (a) they were never treated as citizens prior to the adoption of the Constitution, nor would were they treated as such by Great Britain at that time, and (b) because the Constitution's provision of measures regarding enslaved people did not support their treatment as citizens. This is basically revolving-door logic, as the provisions in the Constitution regarding slavery were there as a direct result of the previous conduct of England and the colonies regarding slavery; the two were not independent. Moreover, he completely ignores the fact that England eventually abolished slavery, as did some states—points that if considered would defeat his basis for holding that Africans and their descendants could not be citizens.

A further glaring inconsistency in Chief Justice Taney's opinion is that he declared that a state could not confer upon Africans US citizenship or citizenship within other states, but he used the statutes and laws existing in the states prior to the adoption of the Constitution as a basis for asserting Africans' comprehensive non-citizenship. In other words, he allowed the state to determine US citizenship if it allowed slavery, but not if it prohibited slavery. This contradiction defies logic, except insofar as to prove the obvious bias of the Chief Justice—and of a majority of the Supreme Court of 1857—in favor of slavery.

Then Chief Justice Taney went further: he cited certain acts of Congress and actions of the president or executive of the US government in support of the proposition that Africans or Negroes were not citizens of the state within the meaning of the Constitution. But again, this is a circular argument, as it is clear that a majority of Congress at the time of the decision in *Dred Scott* were proslavery and that the president at the time was also in favor of slavery. On this basis, though, the Chief Justice argued that the Supreme Court's conclusion that Africans or Negroes were not citizens was required by the other branches of the federal government. This presents another inconsistency: The Constitution sets out each branch of government as coequal, separate and independent of the others, thus the Supreme Court is not bound by the actions of the other branches of government. Yet following Chief Justice Taney's logic, the Supreme Court is almost subservient to the other branches of government, which appears to be wholly inconsistent with the structure and language of the Constitution.

Thus, Chief Justice Taney concluded that given that the Scotts, as Africans or Negroes, were not citizens of the state of Missouri under the federal Constitution, there was no federal diversity jurisdiction for the federal courts to hear and decide the Scotts' case. It appears that he was, precariously, arguing for and against the same point. If the Court has no jurisdiction, that should end the matter; but for the Court to settle the slavery question once and for all, he had to establish that the Court had the ability to answer the questions raised in the case, despite the lack of jurisdiction. He then proceeded not only to give the Supreme Court the ability to reverse the decision of the lower federal court, based on its finding of jurisdiction, but to determine that the Court could correct any other errors in the record. Thus again, the Chief Justice was indicating that the Supreme Court had no jurisdiction or power to hear and decide the case, but that the Court nevertheless would decide the case. While this may seem confusing to the reader, that is exactly what happened. The reason for the confusion is the clear bias of the Chief Justice and the Court toward preserving slavery.

Next, since Scott's claims to freedom rested on the Missouri Compromise, Chief Justice Taney turned to an examination, based on the facts of the case, of whether the Compromise fell within Congressional authority. In dealing with this issue, he advised that the authority of Congress over a particular territory acquired from a foreign government depended upon the power ceded to it at the time the territory was acquired. Moreover, Chief Justice Taney analogized the Bill of Rights provisions, indicating that just as these rights could not be violated within the territories acquired by the federal government, the right of property and the requirement of due process to deprive citizens of property also could not be subject to Congressional action within this territory. Thus, he continued, a slaveholder could not be deprived of his property rights in enslaved people merely through transporting them into a state or territory where slavery had been abolished. The Chief Justice then reiterated that property rights in enslaved persons were comparable to other property rights and that Congress, by enacting the Missouri Compromise to provide that slavery was prohibited in the northern portion of the Louisiana Territory, essentially deprived slaveholders of their property without due process, and therefore the Missouri Compromise was unconstitutional and void.

According to Chief Justice Taney, the invalidation of the Missouri Compromise also foreclosed the Scotts' contention that their travel to land indicated in the Missouri Compromise as free territory made them free. The Chief Justice also advised that even being taken to Illinois was not sufficient to overcome the Scotts' status as enslaved persons, under *Strader*, as the law of Missouri—where slavery was permitted—would determine their status, rather than the law of Illinois, which prohibited slavery. Chief Justice Taney then indicated after careful examination of Missouri law, that the Scotts would remain enslaved persons.

Ironically, Chief Justice Taney even referred to the state court action in which Missouri's highest court reversed and remanded the Scotts' state court case. It is important to note that the Chief Justice did indicate that the lack of jurisdiction was based on the Scotts' proceeding under diversity jurisdiction, which required the case to be brought between citizens of different states. He notes that the Scotts could have sought review by the US Supreme Court of the decision of the Missouri Supreme Court, but that they instead chose diversity jurisdiction. It is debatable whether such a tactical choice would have changed the result of the case, given the Court's nature and its opinion weighing so heavily in favor of slavery's justification and legality.

In addition to the majority opinion issued by Chief Justice Taney, Associate Justice James Moore Wayne authored a concurring statement that Associate Justices Samuel Nelson, Robert Cooper Grier, Peter Vivian Daniel, John Archibald Campbell, and John Catron all joined. As is the case in many landmark decisions, many Justices wanted to weigh in on the case and write separately to address specific matters. It was clear from this fact that, like Chief Justice Taney, the other Justices were keenly aware of the ripple effects this case would have throughout the country. They did not know, nor could they have imagined, the impact this case would have on the history and legacy of the Court.

Like a majority of the Court at that time, Justice James Moore Wayne was a Southerner, from Savanah, Georgia. Justice Wayne ultimately was one of the longest serving justices in the history of the Court. He concurred with Chief Justice Taney's majority opinion and noted that it was stated correctly and appropriately. He specifically indicated his full agreement with the opinion and its conclusions, and indicated that as a result, he would not write a separate opinion. His statement dealt squarely, again, with the issue of jurisdiction, in an attempt to reinforce the position that the Supreme Court could decide the main issue in the case: the Scotts' status as property rather than as citizens and free individuals; and that it could decide the constitutionality of the Missouri Compromise, despite the lack of jurisdiction.

Given the attention that Chief Justice Taney and Associate Justice Wayne placed on the jurisdiction issue, it is apparent that there were some real concerns with the portion of the Court's ruling not dealing with it. This supports the contention that the substance of the *Dred Scott* decision is not good law nor does it have precedential value, a point that scholars still debate. And beyond Justice Wayne's statement, several other members in the majority, although agreeing in principle with his statement, wrote separately regarding specific areas which they sought to advance in the case. A discussion of each and every statement issued by the other Justices in the majority, agreeing with Chief Justice Taney, is beyond the scope of this text. Instead, to summarize, these opinions also dealt extensively with the question of jurisdiction and the Supreme Court's peculiar ability to decide the merits of the case despite the jurisdiction issue. This contributed to the appearance that the Court's majority was committed to a contradiction. It also signaled agreement by these members of the Court that the slavery question should be settled. Of course, despite the Court's efforts, this did not ultimately happen; in fact, the opposite result occurred.

There were two members of the Court who dissented in the case, Associate Justices John McLean and Benjamin Curtis. Both appeared to take issue with the majority's claims regarding jurisdiction. In addition, Justice Curtis dissented on the question of the Scotts' citizenship. Justice McLean specifically examined the previous decisions of the Missouri Supreme Court, in most of the cases prior to that of the state court decision in *Scott v. Emerson*, which he indicated supported the Scotts' claim for freedom.[31] It is telling that even at the Supreme Court level, there was disagreement about the Scotts' cases and, more broadly, about the question of slavery overall.

But in the United States, the Supreme Court's decisions are based on a majority of the Justices, and the majority in this case ruled against the Scotts. If a majority agrees on both the result and the reasoning for the result, the case is decided by a majority opinion, and that opinion becomes precedent, which must be followed by lower courts in future cases in spite of its possible lack of precedential value.

One of the more interesting things about the case and the decision is the coldness and sterility with which the members of the Court talked about the Scotts.[32] There was a clear proslavery slant to the majority opinion, hiding behind intellectual exercises in an attempt to achieve the desired result. The fact that the Court rendered a substantive decision was in and of itself proof that it was attempting to decide a question that was too large for even the Supreme Court to answer.

Understanding the Court's position on slavery in 1857 is challenging. The majority wrestled with the question of slavery from a standpoint of constitutional identity. The dissent, on the other hand, appeared to try to deal more squarely with the facts of the case. It is certainly difficult to grasp the extent to which the Chief Justice attempted to justify the result through history, legal decisions in various slave states, and even by actions of England. No doubt the national and international tensions over slavery were among the Court's background considerations when it rendered its decision. Essentially, the Justices may have taken different routes, but they arrived at the same destination: Dred and Harriett Scott could not change their condition as enslaved persons or obtain their freedom through the federal courts, but rather it was up to the states—in this case, Missouri, which had at that point decided in favor of their continued enslavement.

Not only did the Court indicate that it was powerless to assist the Scotts in the face of contrary state law, the Court claimed that Congress was equally powerless to do so.[33] In fact, one of the greatest unintended consequences of the Court's decision is that it became the first actual concrete target at the federal level for abolitionists and antislavery advocates. This is because it revealed the true ill of slavery: how slavery had so penetrated and permeated American society that this body, the Supreme Court of the United States, was not immune to its affects. Thus, the Supreme Court, the sole expositor of the US Constitution, could not help the Scotts.

Though valiant in their effort and clever in their argument, Dred and Harriett Scott lost... for the time being. It is worth pondering whether the Scotts had a chance at all. Despite precedent, the Supreme Court had become a Jacksonian Court and thus, the result was probably foregone. But the Scotts and their attorneys brought the case anyway. What if the Supreme Court had decided otherwise? Would that have changed the course of history? Would the Civil War have been avoided or perhaps merely accelerated? Would Lincoln have lost the election of 1860, and would his Republican Party have failed to gain control of Congress? All of these are valid questions, and some are wonderful hypotheticals, but they are just that. The facts are that the Supreme Court did not bestir itself to help the Scotts. How much damage the decision caused remains the subject of debate and will be discussed later in this book.

Even if one is not a lawyer or legal scholar or even knowledgeable about the law, one may be familiar with or have heard of the case *Dred Scott v. Sandford.* Quite possibly it was in a civics or social studies class in grade or secondary school or in a US history class in college. This case is an important although unflattering chapter of the legal lexicon of the United States. Despite whatever else Chief Justice Taney, especially, and the other members of the Supreme Court accomplished in their lives and professional careers, they will always be known for this case. This case will always be discussed as the most important part of Chief Justice Taney's legacy, both for him and for his era on the Court. Perhaps the sheer size of this case—the majority opinion, concurrences, dissenting opinions, briefs, and lawyers' summaries—is an indication of its importance. It is clear that the voluminous nature of the documents involved suggests the weight of importance that the Court placed on its decision. Except for Justice Grier, every other Justice on the Court issued an opinion or statement in the case, one way or the other.[34] It is possible that given the state of the nation as it pertained to the issue of slavery, the Court realized that its decision would be heavily scrutinized and dissected and wanted to ensure a thorough record was in front of all who would consider the case in the future.

On the other hand, it is possible that the Court wanted to develop a comprehensive record because it wanted to enshrine and entrench slavery into the fabric of the United States for years and generations to come. Regardless of their intent, the decision of the Court is a part of the Constitutional law canon of the US legal system. The decision became the law of the land under the US Constitution, the Supreme Court having decided not only the fate of the Scotts but the fate of all enslaved persons in the country and even free Africans in Northern territories. This case determined that regardless of whether a Negro was enslaved or free, that person was not and could not become a citizen of the United States, and therefore, that person would receive no protection under the US Constitution. Moreover, by declaring that Congress did not have the power to regulate or prohibit slavery in the territories, the Court essentially—albeit, as it turned out, temporarily—settled the slavery question from a legal standpoint. In that vein, the Court and Chief Justice Taney accomplished their goal. They attempted to answer the question that had plagued this country since well before the American Revolution. In the way they did so, the US Supreme Court once again chose to reinforce the prevailing view of the president—previously Jackson and then at the time of the decision, Buchanan—as well as that of a majority of Congress, as both branches of government were controlled by the proslavery Democratic Party at that time.

Given the extent of agreement among those in power, the decision in its time may not have generated the shock and awe that it has since engendered. Instead, it was likely seen as restoring or maintaining order in the country, settling a divisive issue. As for the actual legal interpretations represented in the decision and whether they pass muster, it is not clear. Reasonable legal minds can disagree, and have, as to the Court's reasoning and justification for the decision.

However, as with most or all Supreme Court cases, the practical affects tend to far outweigh the legal ones. In terms of the legal analysis, the Court's position regarding its ability to decide the case, despite its decision that the Scotts were not citizens and that therefore diversity jurisdiction did not apply, appears tenuous at best. Once the Court determined that the Scotts were not US citizens, the case could have been dismissed without further comment, and the Missouri Supreme Court holding, and subsequent retrial would prevail. This would not have changed the outcome, given the fact that this is where the case as decided by the Supreme Court ended up. In fact, dismissal would have allowed the Court to accomplish its objective without taking the brunt of the blame. As it has done with many cases throughout its history, the Court could have punted the football back to Missouri and blamed it on the slave states or on Congress by virtue of the Missouri Compromise. But the Court chose not to take this easy way out legally. Instead, it saw itself in a greater role.

This leads to the two-pronged central tenet of the Court's decision: enslaved persons' exclusion from the possibility of citizenship by virtue of their status as enslaved persons specifically, or people of African descent in general; and the inability of Congress to prohibit slavery. This conclusion is somewhat more difficult to parse. On one hand, there are very few references to slavery in the Constitution, even though it was clearly debated and discussed during the Constitutional Convention. On the other hand, if there is a body under the Constitution that could regulate slavery at the federal level, it would be Congress.

It remains largely unclear what the most appropriate decision would have been. From a moral standpoint, it is obvious that the decision was wrong, a fact universally acknowledged today. *Dred Scott* ultimately stands as a constant hallmark of the historical weight of slavery in the United States and of the country's relationship with Africans, Negroes, and now African Americans.

CHAPTER 3

THE LEGACY OF DRED SCOTT

The Immediate Aftermath of the Case for the Scotts Personally

The Civil War and the Thirteenth, Fourteenth, and Fifteenth Amendments to the US Constitution all can be traced back in some part to Dred Scott. The cases of Homer Plessy and Rev. Oliver Brown, discussed in the chapters that follow, are both products of Scott's legacy. Thus, even in defeat, his legacy calls out to our current generation about what can happen when one man and one family have the courage to rise up and seek to change their circumstances. Nevertheless, for the parties involved, the Supreme Court's decision was personal and powerful. For the Scotts especially, their long fight, which had begun some three years before, had now come to an end. Both the Missouri Supreme Court and the US Supreme Court had spoken. There were no further appeals to be taken, there was no further legal recourse: they would remain enslaved persons, at least in the eyes of the law.

It has been said that there is no difference between the hero and the coward. The saying goes that they are both frail, flawed characters, both afraid of failure and of getting hurt. But it is what the hero does and what the coward does not do that separates them. Furthermore, courage has been described as doing what is truly in your heart. Feeling the fear and doing it anyway. Based on various accounts, as we have seen, Scott was not a man of great physical stature or strength. Thus, he was not a physical threat like Nat Turner. Nor was he a great orator or public intellectual like Frederick Douglass. Instead, you have this ordinary, unassuming man who wanted a better life and future for his daughters and his family. Yet ordinary as he may have appeared, Scott possessed the one characteristic that is necessary to become a movement mentor: he was courageous. Because of his courage, he acted in the face of great opposition, and his name is now forever etched in the annals of law and history. He had the conviction to continue his quest all the way to the end. After he lost his case at the hands of the Jacksonian Supreme Court, he and his family were sold to his former master Peter Blow's son, Taylor, and they were freed.[1] It is not clear whether they were freed due to the national notoriety that was ultimately garnered by the case. It is not clear that they would not have been freed anyway, as the Blow family was instrumental in obtaining legal counsel and providing funds to support Dred's and Harriett's cases as they moved forward in the courts. In fact, many of the Scotts' lawyers over the years were acquaintances of or hired by the Blow family. It is not clear whether this slaveholding family's personal relationship with Scott changed them or they believed in the cause he represented.

Dred and Harriett Scott continued to live in St. Louis, the state that had denied them their freedom under the law. Then, on September 17, 1858, a little more than a year after the Supreme Court had also denied him his freedom, Dred Scott passed away of tuberculosis.[2] He endured a long and protracted legal battle that likely took a toll on him and his family. Two years before the election of

Abraham Lincoln, the Republican control of Congress, and the start of the bloodiest war in this nation's history, Scott's journey ended.

The Impact of the Case on the Country

But Scott's legacy did not end. It lives on some 160 years later. It lives on in his family as well as his case serving as a shining example of the importance of fighting the fights that need fighting. At first glance, some may regard Scott as a loser, since he lost at both the state and federal levels. But indeed, he was far from a failure. As indicated earlier, while scholars disagree about the extent, it cannot be denied that Scott's case placed slavery on the dashboard of the country. It forced the issue of slavery to the forefront of the presidential and congressional elections of 1860. Because it did, the country remained on a collision course with history and itself. Even if Scott's case was not the final match, at worst his case fanned the flames, and at best it was an early spark, which lit the fires of the abolition of slavery and, eventually, the path toward citizenship in the Thirteenth and Fourteenth Amendments to the US Constitution. It was likely that after Dred Scott, African Americans would be looked at differently in the eyes of history.

It was watched more by the political leaders of the time. The Republicans in Congress used the result in *Dred Scott* to bolster their antislavery platforms in their bid to take control of Congress. In addition, a young senator named Lincoln from Illinois—the direct opposite to the incumbent president, James Buchanan—was beginning to make slavery an important issue in his eventual campaign for president. In fact, slavery was central to his much-publicized debate with Senator Stephen A. Douglas, who was on the opposite side of Lincoln on the slavery issue. The Supreme Court's decision in *Dred Scott* was a signal, a bulwark, a hallmark of the slavery era, as the "peculiar institution" had finally been fully sanctioned by the highest court in the land. It was truly a watershed moment for slavery in the United States.

However, immediately after the decision came down, slavery's future was still uncertain: would it be outlawed, or would it be forever cemented in American society? At the time, the tones of nullification and secession were beginning to crescendo across the country. It would take almost three years, but in the elections of 1860 the Republicans would take Congress, and that young Senator from Illinois would become President of the United States.

The tide began to turn toward abolition. Soon, and for five long years, the country would be embroiled in a bitter civil war between the North and the South. In order to help sway sentiments during the war, and arguably to help win it, President Lincoln issued the Emancipation Proclamation. Thus, enslaved persons in the Confederate states were freed under the law. Within the next eleven years, the Thirteenth and Fourteenth Amendments were ratified, which abolished slavery nationwide and granted citizenship to the formerly enslaved persons. These two constitutional amendments were a direct response to the *Dred Scott* decision. As such, these amendments corrected the Supreme Court's miscarriage of justice in Scott's case. If Scott had not brought the case, it is possible that none of the civil war amendments, the Thirteenth, Fourteenth or Fifteenth Amendments would have come to fruition.

Historians speculate as to whether the effect of the decisions in the Scotts' cases changed the attitudes of African Americans in the North or in the South toward their ability to achieve their freedom. It is also interesting to contemplate whether the case might have changed the attitudes of the country's white majority toward Negroes, particularly given the Court's majority opinion, which contained very harsh language depicting Negroes as property rather than human beings. Let us bear in mind that the constitutional amendments required ratification by the states, where every political process was controlled by the majority. It is entirely possible that those who were on the side of abolition or at the very least not fans of slavery understood the wrongness of the decision in *Dred Scott* and at least were willing to take steps to overturn it through the constitutional amendment. In little more than a decade, property had become people in the eyes of the law. Dred Scott was a big part of that result.

Over the ensuing three years after the decision, the United States was a country in chaos. Various states had adopted differing rules on even speaking about slavery, and congressmen had come to fisticuffs, resorting to violence over it. On top of it all, the *Dred Scott* decision essentially prohibited Congress from keeping slavery out of the northern territories. The Court's decision was hotly debated not only in Congress but across the United States as an example of the idea of slavery going too far.

Very soon, adding chaos of a different order of magnitude, several southern states seceded from the Union, with others considering it. Against this backdrop, Abraham Lincoln was elected president in 1860 amid one of the largest voter turnouts in the nation's young history,[3] and *Dred Scott* had a significant effect on the election. There was division in the South, with Republicans accusing Douglas of favoring the decision when he said that slavery could be extended throughout the territories, without voters or legislatures in those territories having a say in the matter.[4] In fact, during the Lincoln-Douglas debates, Douglas advanced popular sovereignty, or the idea that white male voters should decide the issue of slavery. And he did also express agreement with the *Dred Scott* decision, specifically with Justice Taney's indication that people of African descent were not intended to be citizens but were relegated to the status of property. Moreover, Douglas went further and indicated his opposition to the idea of people of African descent receiving full citizenship. In fact, he went so far as to suggest that those who wanted people of African descent to receive full citizenship should support Lincoln (although that was not exactly Lincoln's entire position on the matter, at least at that time) and the "Black Republican Party," clearly seeking to incense the Democrats in the South around the issue of slavery.[5]

All throughout the South, and the North, blacks and whites had strong opinions about the issue of slavery. Slaveholding Southerners likely used *Dred Scott* to justify or support continuing slavery, and Northern abolitionists likely objected to the case and used it to defend the abolitionist cause. As history would eventually indicate, this gamble by Douglas, the South, and even the majority of US Supreme Court Justices would not pay off. Ultimately, *Dred Scott* aided in plunging the country into the bloodiest and costliest war it has ever seen. Republicans used *Dred Scott* as political fodder. For instance, Sen. John P. Hale of New Hampshire indicated that the Lecompton Constitution (of the state of Kansas—a controversial constitution intended to deal with the issue of slavery in order for Kansas to be admitted as a state) was used as a means of forcing *Dred Scott* on the state of Kansas.[6] Senator William Seward of New York called the *Dred Scott* decision "… judicial usurpation, that is more odious and intolerable than any other among the manifold practices of tyranny."[7] Indeed, the political fallout from the case far outweighed the precedential impact.

In the press, as expected, Republican outlets such as the *New York Tribune*, the *Independent*, the *Ohio State Journal*, and the *Chicago Tribune*, among others, all decried the decision. On the other hand, Democratic outlets such as the *Illinois State Register*, the *New York Journal of Commerce*, the *Richmond Enquirer*, the *Nashville Union* and *American*, the *New Orleans Picayune*, and the *Charleston Mercury* all praised the decision and hailed its result.

Probably the most significant result of the *Dred Scott* decision was the Civil War—or the "War of Northern Aggression," as it was and sometimes still is referred to, especially in the South. Some historians dispute the case's significance given the number of other influences that some contend led the country to war. But if the Civil War was the climax in the American story's chapter on slavery, *Dred Scott* was at least the first act. No story about slavery could be told without reference to Dred Scott. And winning the tug-of-war over slavery was arguably one of the main purposes of both sides in the Civil War.

In the immediate aftermath of the *Dred Scott* decision, something else happened: the country's population began to grow, particularly in the North.[8] It was this growth that increased northern congressional representation and helped Republicans gain control of Congress, along with the White House, which ultimately resulted in actions that led Southern states to secede and eventually to travel down the path to Civil War and its aftermath, Reconstruction.

The Impact of the Case on African American History

African American history in the U.S. can best be described as a journey filled with struggle: the struggle for freedom, identity, legitimacy, and respect. African people in this country had and continue to have a peculiar relationship with the US Supreme Court, as will be further laid out in this book. *Dred Scott* was not the first case to raise the issue of slavery with the Court, but this case was different in that it was by and large a direct attack not only on the institution of slavery but arguably on the structure and function of the US Constitution itself. This is given the characterization of slavery through the fugitive slave clause, as well as the three-fifths compromise, which counted African Americans as three-fifths of a white person for purposes of representation under the Constitution. The *Dred Scott* case stands prominently within the bastion of African American history as well, as it is the confirmation of what many early African Americans experienced throughout the peculiar institution of slavery and understood about the colonization of Africa by countries throughout the world.

It is difficult to discuss African American history without discussing *Dred Scott*. First, this case involved enslaved persons bringing a case in the highest court in the land. Second, it is the story of an attempt by the Scott family to reclaim their humanity and gain their freedom, using the same system that had enslaved them. The struggle of African American people is in many ways a paradox. *Dred Scott* is a constant reminder of the almost four hundred years of slavery endured by African Americans. Perhaps the closest Supreme Court case in terms of the Court's placing its stamp of approval on the inhumane treatment of an entire race of people, is *Korematsu v. United States*, which upheld the internment of Japanese Americans during World War II.[9]

One of the other impacts of *Dred Scott* on African American history was to challenge the premise that African Americans were inferior, to be treated as property, or not deserving of human rights or recognition. *Dred Scott* is a pronouncement to the entire country, and even to future generations, of the dangers of treating any human beings as less than. Prior to the case, various decisions of the US Supreme Court, and even the Constitution itself, left the issue of slavery to be decided among the several states, without establishing a policy on its legitimacy that would apply to the whole nation.

However, once *Dred Scott* was decided, the federal government could no longer stand on the sidelines. Nor hide behind inaction or indifference. Instead, for African Americans, after *Dred Scott*, in the words of Dr. King, the promissory note of freedom issued by the federal government was returned on insufficient funds. Ironically, the decision was in some ways a symbolic victory for African Americans in this country. Moreover, it appeared likely that the decision would help to inspire future generations of people of African descent. Dred Scott's family continues to this day, and they, along with historians, particularly in Missouri, have preserved the history of this case as a shining example of courage and conviction.

The *Dred Scott* decision must also be viewed within the context of contemporary people of African descent's lives at the time. For instance, John Brown's slave rebellion at Harper's Ferry occurred not long after *Dred Scott* was decided. Brown's raid was characterized as creating fear and apprehension among whites in the South, adding to the mood of the country on the issue of slavery. In addition, the Supreme Court's decision in *Dred Scott* only bolstered the case made by the great abolitionist and orator Frederick Douglass. In fact, in the aftermath of the decision, Douglass would remark in a speech in New York that *Dred Scott* was "… a means of keeping the nation awake on the subject… [and that his] hopes were never brighter than now."[10] *Dred Scott* became a rallying cry for those in the abolitionist movement. The case also served as a shining example of the struggle from slavery to freedom. During the Civil War, Negroes who had been freed by the Emancipation Proclamation decided to serve on the side of the Union in order to fight for their freedom, in the spirit of the *Dred Scott* case.

There is little question that *Dred Scott* represented a line in the sand drawn by the Court in terms of African Americans. However, at the same time it became a rallying point. It was clear after *Dred Scott* that the gauntlet had been laid; the die cast. Many enslaved persons were taken through the "Door of No Return" in Ghana. However, through *Dred Scott* case their descendants had entered a different door. This door would either lead to slavery as a permanent condition, or it would be the beginning of the end of slavery.

Ultimately, as history would unfold, the latter would prove to be true, and *Dred Scott* signaled to African Americans that the end of slavery was near. It was the proverbial light at the end of the tunnel. If the struggle to end slavery and seek equality in African American history was a heavyweight fight, *Dred Scott* was an early-round defeat—but not a knock-out, only a technical decision—and the fight was not over. On balance, *Dred Scott* was more than a moral victory, as it started something that began to catch fire all around the country. It represents the hope of an entire race of people. *Dred Scott* became synonymous with change, struggle, and freedom. The freedom struggle could not exist without Dred Scott. There most certainly would be no *Plessy*, no *Sweatt*, no *Loving*, no *Brown*, if it were not for the Scotts. Dred Scott came well before his time. His idea was a foreign concept at the time but would ultimately become the triumphant notion. Dred Scott meant and continues to represent hope for a people, and for the future.

The Legal Legacy of the Case

There is still some debate among legal scholars as to whether and to what extent the most controversial portions of the *Dred Scott* decision are legal precedent. Specifically, as noted in chapter 2, once the Court determined that Dred and his family were not citizens of the United States or of the State of Missouri, then the federal courts and consequently the Supreme Court lacked jurisdiction (or the legal power to hear and decide the case). Thus, the majority opinion, a good portion of it authored by Chief Justice Taney, would be *obiter dictum*, carrying no precedential value. In other words, all of the language in the opinion detailing the history of the country and Negroes, and why they were considered property and not entitled to human or civil rights, would have been merely the Chief Justice's observation and would have no legal value. This would mean that lower courts were not obligated to follow a sizable portion of the majority opinion.

The two justices who joined the majority of the Court in the result, but refused to side with the majority on this issue, Justices Campbell and Nelson, prevented this from serving as precedent anyway, but rather as a plurality opinion.[11] This means that while Sanford won the case, the citizenship portion of the case—along with the more controversial portions of the opinion describing Africans as property and even finding the Missouri Compromise unconstitutional—is likely not precedent.[12] The decision in *Dred Scott* would have such an effect not only on other cases but on the Court itself.

Such a disagreement arose between Chief Justice Taney and Justice Curtis that it led to Justice Curtis's resignation from the Court, effective September 1, 1857.[13] This allowed President Buchanan, a proslavery advocate who fully supported the *Dred Scott* decision, to quickly appoint Nathan Clifford of Maine to succeed Justice Curtis. But many courts would follow *Dred Scott*, just as there would be further cases influenced by it both at the Supreme Court and in other courts across the country. The legal legacy through the courts is evident throughout constitutional history. There are several cases for which *Dred Scott* served as precedent in a legal sense. But as indicated in the previous section, its crux and force as a Supreme Court case also evidenced its limitations.

Furthermore, the Supreme Court failed in its attempt to resolve the issue of slavery.[14] Given the makeup of the US Constitution and republican form of government, it was the Congress that had the ultimate power to address slavery. *Dred Scott* illuminated this fact ever so eloquently. Among all the others, one of the chief criticisms of the decision, is that it did not even accomplish its purported objective. (It is not clear whether Chief Justice Taney shared his views of the matter publicly, although during the Lincoln-Douglas debates, then-candidate Lincoln accused Douglas, President Buchanan, and Chief Justice Taney of taking part in an implicit—if not explicit—conspiracy to ensure that slavery would spread throughout the entire country.) Instead, *Dred Scott* simply exacerbated tensions over the issue of slavery and made it more a focus of contention, politically and morally, than it had been before the case was decided.[15] Perhaps it was the fact that Chief Justice Taney had finally put into words what was implicit in the Constitution and explicit in the slave states and slaveholders throughout the North and South.

For the first time the federal government had officially sanctioned slavery. As a result and enabled by the election in 1864 renewing Republican majorities in the House and Senate, Congress went to work.[16] While all three amendments—the Thirteenth, Fourteenth, and Fifteenth Amendments to the US Constitution—can be said to have been proposed by Congress in response to *Dred Scott*, the Fourteenth Amendment likely owes much of both its origin and its essence to the case. Specifically, the Fourteenth Amendment upon its presentation included a specific change from its original draft. This change was to specifically overrule Chief Justice Taney's opinion that Africans were not and could not be "citizens" within the meaning of the Constitution. This was done through a change proposed in the Senate to Section 1 of the amendment, stating that all persons born in the United States or naturalized are citizens.[17] The purpose of this language was to specifically reverse the *Dred Scott* decision itself, as the Republican majority in Congress saw it as an erroneous decision.[18] Senator Jacob Howard characterized the provision imbuing citizenship on any person born in the United States as an extension of natural and national law. An important part of the reason this was necessary was to ensure that the laws Congress passed to effectuate the amendments affecting formerly enslaved persons would be carried out, particularly in the former Confederate states.

The paradigm of a Supreme Court decision catalyzing Congressional action leading to legislation overturning the decision would become a constant theme throughout the legal and political history of the United States. This is particularly true in the area of civil rights. For instance, after Congress passed the Reconstruction-era Civil Rights Act of 1875, which was designed to prohibit discrimination in public accommodations, employment, and other areas of life, the Supreme Court declared it unconstitutional.[19] Nearly a hundred years later, Congress adopted the Civil Rights Act of 1964, in direct contravention of this decision, this time passing constitutional muster.[20] Given that the Court's decision striking down the first Civil Rights Act stood for nearly a century,[21] *Dred Scott* was not the last time that the US Supreme Court asserted a bar to the rights of people of African descent.

Dred Scott Example Today

Given the politics of the day—the Civil War, the Constitutional Amendments that followed, and Reconstruction—it is difficult to find a Supreme Court decision in recent history that would equal the impact of *Dred Scott*. The case encompassed so much: the Supreme Court's delving into the political spectrum; the nation on the brink of civil war; an entire people of untenable status for whom the national leadership had no plan or idea; and many other elements. Indeed, the case sits at the intersection of law and politics and of the Constitution and the Supreme Court. The closest example in recent history to *Dred Scott*, is *Shelby County v. Holder*, issued in the summer of 2013.[22] This is because this decision lays at the very heart of one of the major victories of the modern civil rights movement.

In order to understand the similarities between *Shelby County* and *Dred Scott*, it is important to first understand the Voting Rights Act of 1965 (VRA). Section 5 of the VRA required preclearance or approval by the US Justice Department for any voting-related legislative changes that would affect the minority vote in specific jurisdictions: those found to have historically prevented or encumbered voting by African Americans.[23] The initial legal challenge in *Shelby County* was for the Supreme Court to invalidate Section 5 of the VRA. However, while this challenge was not successful, the Court did the next best thing, which was to throw out the map used to determine which jurisdictions are subject to the preclearance requirement. The obvious effect, then, was to effectively end preclearance until Congress develops a new map to be implemented by the Justice Department. Given the political volatility in that year and with a divided country and generally a divided Congress, it will take extraordinary work for a new map to be approved any time soon. Thus, a major protection for voting rights was effectively gutted by the US Supreme Court.

It is interesting that between 1857, when *Dred Scott* was decided, and 2013, when *Shelby County* was decided, despite the passage of more than two centuries, the regions of the country on the different sides of these issues regarding race have not changed very much. In addition, similar to state-level legislative action that occurred in the wake of *Dred Scott*, many of the states that had been subject to preclearance began to adopt voter laws after *Shelby County*, including voter identification requirements that would have the effect of disenfranchising minority voters. These laws have been challenged, some with a certain level of success. In other cases, the US Supreme Court has been unwilling to take these cases up or have allowed the new voting restrictions to remain in place. In addition to such restrictions, some states have passed legislative maps redrawing congressional districts in ways that have also had the effect of diluting the minority vote. Many of these changes would not have been allowed or even attempted had the preclearance requirement remained in place.

Instead, these states worked in some cases overnight to pass provisions that would begin to roll back many of the protections that the VRA had initiated. Indeed, in the few elections since the *Shelby County* decision was handed down and preclearance halted, the effect of the decision can be seen in significant ways. These results are not surprising, as this was likely the plan all along. The *Shelby County* decision helped to carry out a long-term strategy of concentrating more power in certain segments of the population and diluting the power of others.

Some have posited that these measures have arisen in reaction to the changing demographics of this country. Current projections indicate the United States is rapidly approaching a time when it will be composed of different races or ethnicities without a single majority. Thus, the measures to restrict voting will help to cement the dominance of one race or culture over others—generally, the white Anglo-Saxon race that has dominated this society since its inception. This is significant in comparison with *Dred Scott*, as one of the central purposes of the Court in that decision was to preserve the race-based slavery system that had persisted since before America declared its independence from Great Britain.

Another important parallel between the *Dred Scott* and *Shelby County* decisions is that in each, the Court appears to have taken on a political issue involving race in a very direct and aggressive manner: slavery in the first; the Voting Rights Act in the second. This is despite the fact that what existed in *Shelby County* did not exist in *Dred Scott*. In fact, Chief Justice Taney and the majority in 1857 attempted to accept the invitation to act and resolve the slavery question given the level of inaction by the Congress and the executive branch of the US Government. By contrast, in *Shelby County*, the Court was actually acting *despite* the deliberate and affirmative action of Congress and the president in their passage and signing into law of legislation reauthorizing the VRA. This legislation was accomplished in a bipartisan manner and included several thousand pages of documents and mountains of evidence to support the reauthorization.

In *Shelby County*, it seemed the Court was attempting to fix something that was not broken, at least in the eyes of Congress and the president. What makes *Shelby County* even more problematic when bearing in mind *Dred Scott* is the fact that generally in cases involving civil rights, the US Supreme Court is reluctant to take on the role of a "super legislature," as described by some justices. In reauthorizing the VRA, the legislature and the executive had acted and spoken with one voice, but it appears that in *Shelby County*, the Court disregarded the facts and evidence provided and substituted its own judgment for that of the other branches. What is most peculiar about this occurrence is that the Supreme Court has in many cases in the past declined to do this very thing. It is worth pondering, at least, why the Supreme Court chose to violate one of its own principles in *Shelby County*.

Another similarity between the cases has to do with the Court's selective focus. In *Dred Scott*, it focused on state laws that prohibited marriage and military service based on race, though there were other states that allowed people of African descent to vote and treated these persons as citizens.[24] In the same way, the Court in *Shelby County* appeared to ignore data beyond those that supported the challenge to the VRA. The argument may be made that this happens to some extent in every case, but that response provides no alleviation of these concerns.

What We Can Learn from Dred Scott Today

Because of its effects on slavery, the African American experience, and civil rights law, *Dred Scott* is discussed and written about more than any US Supreme Court decision other than the other two prominent cases discussed later in this book. Yet there is still much we can learn from *Dred Scott*.

For African Americans, the case stands as proof of what is possible if one does not avoid the struggle. At the same time, it is also a lesson in how to take a defeat. While Scott ultimately was granted his freedom by the descendants of the Blow family, who had owned the Scotts originally, he did not win his case. And unfortunately, due to tuberculosis, his journey did not last much longer. But the fact that a course is not successful does not mean that the fight should not be pursued. The fights that are worth fighting may many times be unsuccessful. While the Scotts lost their battle at the Supreme Court, they ultimately won the war: the South was defeated in the Civil War, and now the three Civil War Amendments stand as reminders of the success that is ultimately attributable to Dred Scott. The *Dred Scott* case reminds us that the race is a marathon rather than a sprint and that sometimes one's leg of the journey is to be the lead-off person, and someone else will be the anchor.

Dred Scott still speaks to us today to help us understand the lengths to which those in power will go in order to maintain that power. Further, he reminds us of the horrors of the institution of slavery and of the necessity of not allowing our society, our nation, or our world to duplicate such atrocities. Anytime we struggle, anytime we fight against injustice and subjugation, we are doing so in the spirit of Dred and Harriett Scott. Furthermore, anytime we refuse to be denied basic human and civil rights and we instead demand to receive equal treatment on the same level and to the same extent as all other people, we are invoking the nature of Dred Scott.

On a very sober and current note, Dred Scott reminds us that although we have come across many rivers, as the saying goes, the world has not been rid of white supremacy, hatred, or racism completely. In 2018 alone, with Charlottesville and other examples, we see that there are still remnants of the sentiment that enslaved an entire race of people. Unfortunately, even today, the words of Chief Justice Taney—that people of African descent and formerly enslaved people had " ... no rights that a white man is bound to respect"[25]—echo across time. We are reminded of these words when we see instances of police brutality and government cruelty targeting people of color, both black and brown. These words are ever to mind when thinking of the portion of the electorate who in 2016 elected Donald Trump to the White House and the over 70 million people who unsuccessfully attempted to send him back to occupy 1600 Pennsylvania Avenue in 2020, with his stated goal to "make America great again." These words from this segment of the population are an eerie reminder of the *Dred Scott* case and the forces behind the Supreme Court's decision.

Dred Scott also reminds us that the courts have not always been the most effective way to fight for social justice and equality. Indeed, in his seminal work, *Where Do We Go from Here: Chaos or Community?*, Dr. Martin Luther King Jr. talked about when using litigation as the sole means of social change, those involved are only passive participants.[26] As a result, the amount of commitment and involvement is not as great as in the case of mass resistance. And as Dred Scott reminds us, due to political concerns and appointments to the federal and state benches, the current courts may not be receptive to the cause of civil rights and social justice. Despite the battle in the courts, the true victories from *Dred Scott* were won in the halls of Congress, through Reconstruction and the passage of the Civil War Amendments.

Today, the US Supreme Court is markedly different from the time of the *Dred Scott* decision. However, it is still a largely conservative Court that has shown a proclivity to rule in favor of maintaining the status quo, either avoiding involvement in matters of race relations or, in many cases, taking a relatively restricted view of these matters. As judicial appointments are being filled through the Senate on a purely partisan basis, like an auto plant assembly line, with little or no debate, the US Supreme Court and other federal courts are becoming more and more conservative. Accordingly, it will be increasingly difficult to seek victories through the federal court system. State courts may be another option, but again, as *Dred Scott* teaches us, litigation, though important, is a limited form of social activism. However, it can bring issues to the forefront and place even egregious results in court on the dashboards of citizens and elected officials. Sometimes litigation can influence elections, and eventually it may bring about change in the laws for the better.

Furthermore, by making the argument in court, it may be possible to spark a dissenting opinion that eventually forms the basis for overturning the current precedent. In *Dred Scott*, the dissents of Justice Curtis and especially Justice McLean were very important. As discussed, such dissent helped to prevent some of the precedential value of the majority opinion. But even more than that, it provided a basis for those opposed to the majority opinion in *Dred Scott* to formulate a reasoned argument against its result. Many abolitionists and opponents of slavery could use these arguments to lessen the *Dred Scott* decision's weight and effect on current and future generations.[27]

CHAPTER 4

THE ACTIVIST: HOMER PLESSY

Why Homer Plessy?
The South after the Civil War

Now under a Republican president who had campaigned on the abolition of slavery and a Republican-controlled Congress that had recently prevailed, albeit barely, in the Great War, the South was reeling from its defeat. The southern states would have to figure out how to deal with rejoining the Union and having the parameters set by Lincoln and the Congress jammed down their throats.

But the South was not easy. It never was. There were southern universities in ruins, and the flames were still felt in some southern cities, thanks to General Sherman. Legislatures that had once voted to secede now had to be forced to adopt state constitutions that adhered to the federal constitution and respected the rights of all citizens equally, including formerly enslaved persons. In the case of many southern states, such words were toothless tigers. Although many danced to the music of the Republican Congress, they maintained their rebel strongholds in the South.

One of the enduring questions about the South after the Civil War surrounds the relatively uncircumscribed nature of reintegration of the forces of rebellion and resistance into the Union. Generally, after one side loses a war, there is some great cost: some land lost, some monetary price to be paid, or some other step that signifies the loss. But in the South, the price of defeat in the Civil War was different. Outside of the tremendous loss of life on both sides, which cannot be understated, many southern landowners who had been slaveholders maintained their strongholds. And many of those who had fought and argued vigorously against the Union before and during the war left the battlefield and eventually went into their states' legislative halls.

Reconstructing the Nation

Among the most pressing items on the Congressional Republicans' list related to the former Confederate states was ratification of the Civil War Amendments, sometimes referred to as the Reconstruction Amendments. As discussed in chapter 2, these are the Thirteenth, Fourteenth, and Fifteenth Amendments to the US Constitution. Their importance in the Homer Plessy story is discussed below. In the wake of *Dred Scott,* the Civil War, the loss by the South, and the victory of Lincoln and the Republicans, including a second term for President Lincoln, these amendments became the hallmark of Reconstruction. Essentially, in many cases, it was ratification of the Reconstruction Amendments that made the former Confederate states' readmission to the Union possible.

Thus, begrudgingly, and likely with great angst, these amendments were ratified one after the other between 1865 and 1870. The span 1865 to 1877 is what historians have designated as the period of Reconstruction of the Union following the Civil War. Notably during this period, there were active efforts by the federal government to ensure that people of African descent and formerly enslaved people would become full citizens of the United States. Even the franchise was provided to African American males, (as women were not granted the franchise, until the ratification of the 19th Amendment). There were several other initiatives that would enhance and seek to fulfill the vision of a united nation, not only in terms of the people of African ancestry and whites but of the South and the North. Like any reconciliation, however, it was not always smooth. It was during this process that Lincoln was assassinated. Andrew Johnson, vice president at the time, would succeed to the presidency. But President Johnson was not a Lincoln supporter, and he was a southerner born in North Carolina and elected from Tennessee. He did not share Lincoln's vision for Reconstruction, and as a result he vetoed some of the legislative acts of Congress—still in Republican hands—including those that were passed to help people of African descent receive and enjoy their full civil and human rights. As a result of the growing tension between President Johnson and the Congress, as well as the alleged violation of the Tenure of Office Act, Johnson became the first president in US history to be impeached, although he was not removed from office.

The Rise of Jim Crow

There were significant strides made in the era of Reconstruction. Congress created the Freedman's Bureau, its programs designed to help people of African descent to invest in American society. Congress also passed certain criminal laws, to help protect people of African ancestry from the tyranny that arose after the Civil War. This was particularly important with the rise of outfits like the Ku Klux Klan, seeking to do through force, murder, terrorism, and intimidation what General Lee and the Confederate Army could not do in the Civil War. The aim of the Ku Klux Klan and others working individually and sometimes collectively was to place fear in the hearts and minds of people of African ancestry. This period was one of the ugliest in our history, when lynching began to rise in the South and across the country. This form of brutal murder was one of the key methods used by these groups to threaten people of African ancestry with violence, along with castration, rape, physical beatings, whippings, and other forms of cruelty.

The Turning of the Tide

Unfortunately, as Congressional Republicans who were responsible for the Civil War Amendments began to fade out and Southern Democrats began to gain in both physical and political power, like the biblical children of Israel, there arose a President and Congress who knew not Lincoln, or Congressman Thaddeus Stevens, or Senator Lyman Trumbull, or others who were pivotal in the abolition of slavery, the establishment of equal protection of the laws, and enfranchisement of African American males. In addition, as a sign of things to come, as early as 1873 President Ulysses S. Grant abandoned federal enforcement of civil rights law in the South and even pardoned many convicted KKK terrorists.[1]

Furthermore, the new justices appointed to the US Supreme Court were not major supporters of the federal government's active fight to protect the rights of the formerly enslaved people in the South. As the pendulum began to swing away from protection for African Americans, toward noninvolvement, and then to complete abandonment, the South took note. Southern states began electing governors who were very outspoken about restricting the rights of African Americans, and southern legislatures began to pass discriminatory laws. In addition, southern state constitutions, which had been required to include protections for all people for readmission to the Union, were now being altered to include discriminatory provisions. Unfortunately for African Americans, the tide began to turn away from them, and not only in the South.

Just as the election of 1860 was a high point for African Americans, the presidential election of 1876 would be an almost equally low point for them. The Republican candidate for president, Rutherford B. Hayes, lost the popular vote to the Democratic candidate, Samuel J. Tilden. Congressional Republicans, however, did not want to give up the presidency, so they worked out a compromise with Democrats during the Electoral College vote in Congress that came to be known as the Hayes-Tilden Compromise of 1877. It would provide the Republicans with the White House, in exchange for the Democrats receiving removal of federal troops from the South, thereby allowing the southern states, and the former Confederacy, to essentially return to pre–Civil War form—but this time with the blessing of the Union.

This development is indicative of the struggle of African Americans in America, where the triumph or perceived triumph is generally cut short when the mainstream American agenda, or that of the white dominant culture, requires that the needs of African Americans once again be placed in the background. This is seen during the Lincoln presidency and passage of the Civil War Amendments, as they were quickly followed by the incremental erosion of their significance year after year. It took only roughly twelve years from the ratification of the Thirteenth Amendment abolishing slavery until the removal of federal troops from the South by Congress in the Hayes-Tilden Compromise. Slavery had lasted for 246 years, and Reconstruction lasted only 12: a stark contrast, but one that many at that time did not recognize.

Just twelve years into Reconstruction, many among the leadership of the country declared that this was long enough. From the US Supreme Court to the halls of Congress, leaders had all but decided that the formerly enslaved Africans no longer needed the assistance of the federal government for them to emerge from the institution of slavery, which itself had lasted almost two and a half centuries. Therefore, the important and really meaningful work of Reconstruction that began after the Civil War was cut short too soon.

This change in the character of the federal government would become a pattern throughout history. This is clear, for example, in the differences between the decisions in two Supreme Court cases, both titled *Brown v. Board of Education of Topeka, Kansas* which will be discussed later in this book. *Brown I* in 1954 provided a victory against segregation in public schools; but *Brown II*, issued within the next year, essentially restrained the force and effect of *Brown I* by allowing desegregation to be implemented as slowly as possible. This tendency can be seen even today with the abandonment of such measures as the Voting Rights Act, which was all but halted by the 2013 Supreme Court decision in *Shelby County v. Holder*, as discussed in chapter 3, coupled with the failure on the part of the other two federal branches to move forward with a legislative fix in response to that decision. The African American freedom journey has been replete with examples of defeat snatched from the jaws of victory. Thus, the post-Reconstruction period is a seminal moment among the reversals of support for African American freedom and equality prior to the *Plessy* case—which, as we will see, upheld the constitutionality of racial segregation under a doctrine of "separate but equal" some twenty years after the end of Reconstruction. The unfinished nature of Reconstruction is possibly just as much a result of this kind of change of course as of the perspective of Lincoln and the Congressional Republicans' vision of reclaiming the Union at all costs. The catalyst could be, then, the failure of the Civil War victors to adequately and appropriately address the Confederacy due to Lincoln's strong desire to preserve the Union. This desire to reestablish the Union outweighed any desire to assist African Americans to achieve true freedom and equality after the Civil War.

As a result, the South would "rise again," Reconstruction would end, and many of the legislative victories that people of African ancestry had received would become merely moral victories, or justice "on paper," but in practice these victories would no longer remain. It is against this backdrop—after the end of Reconstruction, and the re-enshrinement of the forces behind slavery, in the South and elsewhere, as a dominant force to rule over people of African descent—that early activists began to rise. One of these early activists would be a man whose name would be spoken throughout the annals of US legal history: Homer Plessy.

Who Is Homer Plessy?

Ancestry and Heritage

Homer Adolph Plessy was born to Adolphe Plessy and Rosa Debergue, on March 17, 1862, in New Orleans, Louisiana.[2] He was of Creole and Haitian heritage and was described as one-eighth African ancestry and seven-eighths Caucasian.[3] His parents, residents of New Orleans, were free Creole-Haitians. With a strong French and Haitian ancestry and among a sizable New Orleans Creole community, he grew up primarily speaking French. Most Creoles of New Orleans had been free prior to the Civil War, and even afterward—during Reconstruction—many were prominent both in their community and around the state. This ancestry is largely what helped to spur a group of 18 forward-thinking men known as the Comite des Citoyens (Committee of Citizens)[4] and Homer Plessy to seek action. Unlike Dred Scott and his descendants, Plessy's ancestors enjoyed a certain level of freedom and equality. Thus, in his time, the transition back to segregation had not been the recent norm.

Passing for White

Homer Plessy reportedly appeared white to most people, due largely to his Creole ancestry. He was not alone, however, as this was common in New Orleans during that time. As a result, Plessy could "pass" as white. *Passing* is a term that has been applied by people of African descent for many years, both during and after slavery and continuing through the time of the modern Civil Rights movement of the 1950s and 1960s.

Passing was used by people of African descent sometimes as a protective measure, like that of a chameleon to hide in plain sight. Some African Americans used their white-like appearance to avoid discrimination, shame, violence, and other forms of oppression to survive being a person of color in the United States. Some in the modern civil rights era used passing to go undercover to expose racial injustice and violations of civil and human rights. They used passing in order to serve as "double-agents," infiltrating the KKK or other groups bent on committing acts of violence against people of African descent. These infiltrators would report such conduct to their communities, helping them avoid dangers that awaited them. Plessy could likely have lived most of his life in secret, posing as a white person and enjoying the privileges thereof.

Instead, following his Haitian heritage and his fellow Creole community, he chose to resist and challenge the growing tide of what became known as Jim Crow segregation or de jure (by law) across the country, and particularly in the South. In addition, he was influenced by his ancestors and his stepfamily who were very active in the community and engaged in their own form of activism. But Plessy was not alone. The Citizens' Committee was formed to address and challenge many of the laws that were passed in the South to restrain and prohibit people of African descent from enjoying the very freedoms that the Civil War and Reconstruction laws and amendments were designed to create. The Citizens' Committee had a history of using the court system to attempt to create change and sought to mount legal challenges that would end up in the US Supreme Court. Perhaps they considered Homer's appearance to be an advantage for a case of this magnitude and Plessy eventually joined the Citizens' Committee. Plessy's appearance likely made him less susceptible to violence during a protest. Moreover, in Plessy's particular case, not only did he appear white, but he also actually had only one-eighth African ancestry.

When the Citizens' Committee decided it was time to challenge the Louisiana Separate Car Law, which it eventually did, the members particularly liked the fact that Homer had such a small percentage of African heritage. Quite possibly they believed his appearance would also help to create empathy among observers of the case. Their hope was that Homer's appearance would help point out the absurdity of the segregationist laws, that drew distinctions with such minor differences in color and race, for no logical reason beyond the prejudices of the day.

Family Life

Homer's father, Adolphe, passed away when he was seven years old.[5] Two years later, his mother married Victor M. Dupart, a shoemaker, who would help raise Homer.[6] His stepfather's profession was the principal reason Plessy eventually chose shoemaking as his primary profession. He also worked at various times as a laborer, insurance agent, and clerk. These were common professions during this period in the South, although Plessy likely enjoyed closer to a middle-class standard of living in New Orleans.

Homer's life was like that of many in the New Orleans Creole community of the late 1800s. He was moderately educated and had never been enslaved, as his grandparents which included both French and free persons of color emigrated from Haiti. After the Civil War and Reconstruction, many states, including Louisiana, adopted progressive laws and constitutional provisions to guarantee equality to newly freed and formerly enslaved African people.

Plessy married Louise Bordenave on July 14, 1888, at St. Augustine's Church in New Orleans.[7] The couple lived in an integrated middle-class neighborhood, at 244 North Claiborne Avenue. They raised their children, and their descendants live on today.

The Significance of Homer Plessy's Origins
Haiti as the Conscience of the World

It is possible that Plessy's origins provide a clue to his activism. Haiti has sometimes been referred to as the conscience of the world. This island nation has a peculiar history with race and oppression as well. Haiti and African Americans in the United States have a storied history and connection. It was the Haitian revolution that helped to spark and influence Africans in the US South to believe they too could be free and, in some cases, to achieve their own freedom from slavery. When word spread of Haitian people obtaining their freedom from the oppression of colonial rule and securing their own independence, it was inspirational for Africans enslaved in the United States. And for their part, many Haitians relocating to the United States found in New Orleans something akin to an Ellis Island in New York. Thus, it was not uncommon for New Orleans residents to have Haitian heritage and roots.

As might be expected, many of the cultural influences of Haiti—from music, to religion, to art—had a profound effect on the cultural scene of New Orleans. Historically, Haiti was a former territory of France, as Louisiana had been prior to the Louisiana Purchase.

The fact that Louisiana is even a part of the United States is tied to the decision by Napoléon Bonaparte of France to sell the Louisiana Territory to the United States for $15 million. This was largely seen as a direct result of his losing efforts to maintain French rule over Haiti, due to the costs of the Haitian revolution. The island's uprising, then, led to the Louisiana Purchase, doubling the size of the Unites States, at that time. Recognition of this fact contributed to a strong resonance between Haiti and New Orleans, and that connection was demonstrated by Plessy and many Haitian-Creole residents during his time.

Toussaint L'Ouverture and the Haitian Revolution

François-Dominique Toussaint L'Ouverture is regarded as one of the greatest generals and military leaders in world history. This leader of the Haitian revolution engineered one of the largest military upsets ever recorded when he—a formerly enslaved person under the French empire—obtained freedom, returned to lead his people, ultimately defeated Napoléon, and freed his nation. His brilliant military strategy of capturing French soldiers and forcing them to train Haitian soldiers to defeat the French was a major factor in his success. It was one of the great liberation narratives of the world, and to this day, Haiti, despite the nation's financial struggles and natural disasters, remains a free and independent nation.

Haiti still holds a special place for African Americans and people of color in the United States, representing an early story of struggle and persistence in overcoming European aggression and colonialism. Haiti is a reminder that slavery was not unique to the United States, but that US slavery in some ways differed from slavery in other parts of the world, including Haiti. Haitian influence is significant not only in the life and culture of New Orleans but also in the life of Homer Plessy. His grandfather, on his father's side,

Germaine Plessy, a French-born white man fled from Haiti, after it was freed from Napoleon's rule, to New Orleans along with Homer's great-uncle, Dominique in the 1790's.[8] It is no coincidence that the success of General L'Ouverture and the Haitian revolution, would indirectly lead to Homer winding up in New Orleans, and that he would eventually help spur a legal challenge all the way up to the US Supreme Court seeking equality and freedom for African Americans.

Life in New Orleans at the Turn of the Century

By the end of Reconstruction, life in Louisiana was much like life in the rest of the South and a good portion of the North, with segregated schools and public accommodations. Reconstruction laws that were designed to protect African Americans were stripped of their effectiveness, thanks in large part to legal interpretations by state and federal courts in those states that had the effect of restricting the rights of African Americans. Further, not only did many of these judicial decisions rely on narrow legal interpretations, but such interpretations were largely and sometimes exclusively based on racist and white supremacist notions of African American inferiority.

Despite these limitations and lack of success in the courts, the African American community in New Orleans was in many ways middle class, with such occupations as lawyers, doctors, and journalists.[9] During this period, African Americans had a modicum of wealth in New Orleans. The Citizens' Committee was largely made up of people from various white-collar professions and, more importantly, descendants of Creole people who were free prior to the Civil War.[10] The members of the Citizens' Committee comprised a portrait of New Orleans during this time: proud, entrepreneurial, outspoken people with courage to stand up for themselves and for their people, even in the South. It should come as no surprise, then, that the desire, determination, and will, to challenge the Louisiana Separate Car Law all the way to the nation's highest court, arose out of this community.

Early Activist Group

Given the federal government's abandonment of people of African descent in the South for purely political reasons, and the desire of Southern politicians and former slaveholders to return them to as near their previous condition of servitude as possible, Negro people began to see the need for resistance and a means to challenge this new form of oppression. The federal government decided that it was out of the business of using the law to help African Americans rise out of the shadow of slavery. Thus, post-slavery African Americans realized that the legislative branch was only one possible means of overcoming oppression and helping themselves in their effort for freedom. They could not wait for the torch to be passed from Dred Scott, Nat Turner, or Frederick Douglass. When they were ready, they grabbed the torch from the previous generation. The decision to unite and challenge laws such as the Separate Car Law in Louisiana was a tremendous step for an African American community in the wake of the horrific institution of slavery.

What did Homer Plessy Do?

Sitting Down before Rosa Parks

Homer Plessy's action was not motivated by personal ambition or self-serving interests. No, his action was done with the express purpose of challenging immoral and unjust laws like that pertaining to segregated rail cars in Louisiana. He and the Citizens' Committee's plan would eventually become known as "testing," or a staged protest. Before Rosa Park's decision to keep her seat on a bus in Montgomery, Alabama, and before parents brought lawsuits challenging the constitutionality of segregated schools, Plessy and the Citizens' Committee decided to directly challenge Jim Crow laws. These laws were designed to keep Africans, Negroes, or people of African ancestry as second-class or inferior to whites or people of European ancestry. Plessy understood what was happening. He and the Citizen's Committee understood the importance of bringing national attention to individual injustice. They understood the idea of social justice and activism as means of changing the laws. They also understood what Dr. King would later talk about in his *Letter from a Birmingham Jail*: the importance of challenging a law that is unjust, the necessity to do so, and the willingness to be arrested as a form of protest of such unjust law.[11]

When it came time for direct protest of the Louisiana Separate Car Law, Plessy and the Citizens' Committee had almost every detail planned. This included which car to use, and they would even hire a detective to arrest Homer afterward to ensure that the sheriff or other law enforcement would not intervene. After months of planning, they were finally ready to spark a movement.

On June 7, 1892, just as planned, Plessy entered the "whites only" train car that was traveling from New Orleans to Covington, Louisiana, on the East Louisiana Railway and sat down. After he refused to leave, he was arrested by the hired detective, Officer Chris C. Cain, and charged with the crime of violating what was known as the Separate Car Law.[12] His bail was set at $500, and his trial was held on October 28, 1892.[13] Plessy's deed was done. Now he and the Citizens' Committee could directly challenge his charge and consequently the law itself. Plessy's appearance, multicultural background, and the fact that he was only one-eighth black were important in challenging the law. This is because his background helped avoid arguments and distinctions among various colors and classes of race. Instead, it forced the law to be challenged based on its merits, which was the goal of Plessy and the Citizens' Committee.

Challenging the System

The system challenged by Plessy and the Citizens' Committee began in 1619, when the first African people were brought to the North American colonies and enslaved. Essentially, the system of segregation during Plessy's time, was the child of slavery and white supremacy. Enacted in 1890, the Louisiana Separate Car law required separate accommodations in transportation for blacks and whites. Thus, this law was an extension of the notion that Africans or Negroes were somehow inferior and should not mix with or even ride in the same railcar with whites. Plessy and the Committee took a stand, realizing that similar laws had been passed in other states, especially in the South. Moreover, they understood that if Negroes were to ever fully enjoy the purported freedoms they had been promised by the Reconstruction Amendments, they would have to take it upon themselves to challenge the government to live up to them. For them, the true measure of citizenship would not exist until Negroes were able to live, travel, and engage in any other activities of everyday life in the same way and through the same means as whites.

The fact that Plessy and the Committee could strategically and methodically challenge Jim Crow segregation in an orderly, non-violent, and structured way, in and of itself, is proof of the falsity of Negro inferiority.

A Losing Cause

"The fight we are making is an uphill one … [but] perhaps it is best that the battle be fought."[14] These were words spoken by Louis Martinet, a New Orleans attorney who, like Plessy, was a member of the Citizens' Committee, had Creole ancestry, and was light-skinned in complexion. He was referencing the planned challenge to the Separate Car Law in Louisiana; which Plessy would execute. Convinced that the time for inaction had long passed, members of the Citizens' Committee realized, rightfully, that since the President and Congress had abandoned them, their means to freedom and full humanization and recognition resided in their own hands and feet. The revolution would not come from Washington, DC, but would have to start in New Orleans Parish, Louisiana.

Given the conditions of the South, they knew that their campaign would be a longshot. They watched states actively refuse to protect or worse conspire to restrict, the rights of African Americans, through laws like the Separate Car Law in Louisiana. In addition, much like today, federal and state courts did not appear willing to assist African Americans in achieving any gains in race relations. Foreboding the Supreme Court decision in *Plessy v. Ferguson*, federal and state courts essentially were already applying the rule of separate-but-equal prior to it being laid down from on high.[15]

In addition, during this time, the US Supreme Court's recent interpretations of the Thirteenth and Fourteenth Amendments were very narrow, and not indicative of the Court's receptivity to using these amendments to protect the rights of African Americans (to be discussed in the next chapter). Thus, the Citizens' Committee had ample reason to believe that theirs was a lost cause. Nevertheless, they persevered and pressed on even though the African American community had been previously unsuccessful in seeking legal relief in the Courts.[16]

Where Is the Historical Homer Plessy Now?

In New Orleans, at the corner of Press and Royal Streets, a plaque is displayed bearing the case name *Plessy v. Ferguson*. Like many other historical markers, it is there to teach new generations about the significance of historical figures. But it is doubtful there could be a plaque large enough to fit all the words needed to describe Homer Plessy, the Citizens' Committee, and what they accomplished with their lives and their activism. Plessy's plaque represents an entire generation of activists and at the same time a generation of Jim Crow segregation. This is because Plessy's activism not only resulted in a negative decision, but, unfortunately, that decision became the basis for legalized discrimination against African Americans for almost the next half century. It would be impossible to get all the people whom Plessy touched onto a single plaque. It would be difficult to encapsulate on a single plaque what Plessy's case meant to this country.

Homer Plessy was and still is an important historical figure in our society. The plaque as well as the case law, scholarship, and general literature that discuss his case bear this out. Like all historical figures, Plessy receives a somewhat lofty persona. But like many other historical figures, he could not have imagined the impact that his case would ultimately have on generations of African Americans that would follow. Instead, he was likely more concerned with the battles of his day and the struggles and triumphs that he could achieve for himself, his family, his community, and possibly his race.

But the historical figure should not overshadow the human being: his wants, desires, needs, family circumstance, lineage, background, and all the other things that make us up as complex beings. Homer Plessy was likely just as conflicted as most of us are. He was faced with deciding between comfort and convenience, on one hand, or challenge and controversy, on the other. Whatever frustrations he may have felt, whatever fears and apprehensions may have affected him, all should be considered. And as with any such figure, the context in which he lived should always be top of mind. His environment, the temperature of the society that he lived in, the nation, even the world that surrounded him—all these things play a significant role in Homer Plessy's story and the narrative that forms the basis for his status as a historical figure.

The Case that Bears His Name

Homer Plessy's name will forever be associated with the US Supreme Court case that bears it. This case was cited as precedent for almost fifty years; and then, even more than sixty years after it was overturned as precedent, it has continued to be cited and raised as an example of jurisprudence that many in the law would soon forget. Nevertheless, his name is included in the pantheon of civil rights and constitutional law cases. Law students, law professors, and lawyers from around the country and perhaps the world continue to debate and discuss his case and its merits. Even outside the law, many laypersons with knowledge of civil rights history learn about his case. One of the purposes of this book is to hopefully help readers learn from Plessy's case as an example for their own activism.

Both because of the importance of the case at the time it arose and because of the span of time that it ruled the day in this country, *Plessy v. Ferguson* is one of the more recognizable Supreme Court cases even in popular culture or discourse. It is likely surpassed only by the other two cases discussed in this book in terms of its significance in African American history and indeed in US history.

Birth of a Civil Rights Movement

Before there was a Southern Christian Leadership Conference, a National Urban League, a National Association for the Advancement of Colored People, or a National Action Network, there was the Citizens' Committee. Whether they realize it or not, all these civil rights organizations are offspring of early groups like the Citizens' Committee. These were like-minded individuals of color who sought to change the conditions of their people, as they saw them. They refused to stand idly by and watch as former slaveholders turn back the clock from Reconstruction to try to create an environment as close to slavery as possible.

The Committee and Plessy, whether they realized it or not, were birthing a civil rights movement. If there had never been a *Plessy v. Ferguson*, *Brown v. Board of Education* would not have been necessary. The Committee's and Plessy's actions—organizing Plessy's arrest for violation of the Louisiana Separate Car Law—was the beginning of the mass-protest, civil disobedience–oriented, nonviolent movement that became the foundation of the modern American civil rights movement of the 1950s and 1960s. Moreover, Plessy's act directly challenging segregation provided a blueprint for future generations of civil rights leaders even as it recalled other kinds of strategic actions that had been deployed by African Americans throughout their history to fight against oppression.

The modern civil rights movement was not a random, spontaneous protest by several divided groups coincidentally acting in concert. Instead, it was a coordinated, systematic attack with almost military precision. Plessy and the Committee's planned challenge of the Separate Car Law was an early instance of this type of strategy. Utilization of the court system as a tool to dismantle segregation is an approach that future generations would also adopt. The idea of using litigation to seek change, however, did not originate in the Citizens' Committee but had been used previously by abolitionists in the North.

Similarly, the result in *Plessy v. Ferguson* was instructive to future civil rights leaders, as it once again proved that litigation as a tool was limited in its effect on societal norms, and that the personal prejudices of individual judges and Justices deciding such cases would play a role. Thus, leaders of the Modern Civil Rights

Movement recognized the value of mass protest alongside litigation as effective means of challenging segregation and inequality.

Plessy v. Ferguson was decided while the country was in the midst of a rise in white supremacy, seeking a return to earlier times of the suppression of African Americans. In the face of this change and negative sentiment, with lynchings occurring throughout the country, Homer Plessy and the Citizens' Committee persevered. Although the act of resistance likely got most of the local and national attention given its result, Plessy and the Committee were involved in many other types of activities. They realized that it was important to formulate not only a strategic attack but a multilevel approach—to seek equality in schools, in public accommodations, in civic engagement, and in other areas of life and society. They realized that to achieve full citizenship rights in the United States they must attack on all these fronts. This was another aspect of the blueprint for the Modern Civil Rights Movement, whose leaders and participants would also formulate their challenge to segregation in different ways.

CHAPTER 5

A CASE OF CONSCIENCE: *PLESSY V. FERGUSON*

Legal Landscape since Dred Scott

Dred's Descendants

Before the time of the *Plessy* case, the US Supreme Court, like Congress and the rest of Washington, had undergone a tremendous shift. As the tide began to turn away from civil rights for people of African descent across the country, so did the Court. Although it is arguable that the Court had not been instrumental in protecting civil rights up to that time, the *Dred Scott* decision is a perfect example of this.

After the Civil War, with the election of a Republican majority in Congress and a Republican president, Supreme Court appointees were largely from the North. These members included Chief Justice Morrison Waite and Justices Stephen Field, Samuel Miller, and Joseph Bradley.[1] It would appear from the outside that these Justices would be more sensitive to the cause of abolition if for no other reason than to remove the stain of *Dred Scott* from the Court's history. Also, one might expect this Court to seek to protect the recently enacted Civil War Amendments and other Acts passed by Congress during Reconstruction. Alas, as illustrated below, these expectations went largely unmet.

However, not all early decisions were unfavorable for African Americans in the US Supreme Court. For instance, in *Strauder v. West Virginia*, the Court struck down a West Virginia Law restricting the rights of blacks in serving on juries.[2] However, despite this victory, the Court soon began to once again restrict rather than expand the rights of people of African descent, despite the fact that it was interpreting laws that had been enacted for the express purpose of strengthening the rights of African-Americans toward full realization of the benefits of citizenship and participation in society.

Thus in 1873, in the *Slaughterhouse Cases*, the US Supreme Court indicated that under the US Constitution, states did not have to respect fundamental economic and civil rights; instead, the federal government was only prohibited from abridging such rights.[3] This was a tremendous blow to the legal protections afforded to African Americans. This decision essentially limited the federal government's ability to proactively enforce civil rights protections. The decision relegated the federal government to a merely defensive posture regarding civil rights. For instance, the Civil Rights Act of 1875, was seen by many as the hallmark of Congressional Reconstruction. It prohibited discrimination against African Americans in public accommodations. Perhaps forecasting the result in *Plessy*, in the *Civil Rights Cases*, decided in 1888, the US Supreme Court struck down the Civil Rights Act of 1875 as unconstitutional by a margin of eight to one, with Justice John Marshall Harlan Sr. as the lone dissenter.[4]

Like other members of the Supreme Court at the time, Justice Samuel Miller did not believe in the broad national power of the federal government to enforce civil rights laws.[5] In other words, the

Supreme Court during *Plessy* believed that the Fourteenth Amendment was not a sword to enforce rights, but that it was a shield (barely) to protect rights. The striking down of the Civil Rights Act of 1875 is case in point.[6]

Justice Bradley also supported the decline of federal government involvement in the South. He went further, arguing that African Americans should not be treated as a "special favorite" of the laws and should not need the benefit of legislation for them to enjoy full citizenship.[7] One must pause and ask the question, how is it that a race goes from slavery and property, in 1857, in *Dred Scott*, to a "special favorite" of the laws in 1888, roughly thirty years later? The irony in the arguments by Justice Bradley and others is that these same arguments were repeated later, during the civil rights movement of the 1960s, as a basis for resisting the expansion of civil rights protections. In fact, these arguments are still used even today as an excuse for rolling back certain civil rights protections, such as in *Shelby County v. Holder* and other in race discrimination-related cases. It seems that whenever the Supreme Court wished to get out of the business of expanding civil rights protections, this rationale was used. It should have been no surprise, then, given the tenor of the Supreme Court and the Congress, that the Jim Crow Segregation enthusiasts in the South and the North, felt emboldened to rise against the rights of African Americans once again.

Southern Democracy

Southern democracy after the Civil War was much like it would be during the Jim Crow South, or even as it is to this day. Proponents of Dixie, the old Confederacy, or whatever name with which one chooses to identify those states that seceded from the Union and battled its forces during the Civil War, bemoaned the fall of the South, while still others, more skeptical, contend that the South never truly fell even after General Lee's surrender to General Grant in the McLean House near Appomattox, Virginia. Even so, there are some aspects of the Old South that had to yield to the Union's victory.

The most glaring sign of the South's defeat was the abolition of slavery and the ratification of the Thirteenth, Fourteenth, and Fifteenth Amendments to the US Constitution. As discussed in earlier chapters, these events ushered in the Reconstruction period, during which the federal government acted to ensure that the formerly enslaved people of African descent would become full citizens. However, Reconstruction was not long-lived, and by the late 1800s and certainly at the turn of the twentieth century, signs of the fall of the South were much harder to find. There were former Confederates in positions of power politically, socially, and economically. There was still a large agrarian society, and—despite the brief period of relief from 1865 to 1877—yes, people of African descent were once again being oppressed and abused in the South and throughout the country. Sometimes in chains, due to convict leasing, sometimes through violence in the form of lynchings and other acts of terrorism committed by the KKK and others. African Americans were once again subjected to inhumane treatment at the hands of Southern whites. This is not to suggest that such activities did not occur in the North; of course, they did. But the South's unique history with slavery and its messy and bloody divorce from it resulted in the birth of one of its children, namely Jim Crow. As a result, Southern democracy followed suit, with discriminatory laws in education, in public accommodations, and—even where there were constitutional protections—in voting, jury service, and other areas of civic participation. In addition, such laws and practices were mostly upheld in state and federal courts, which were themselves filled with former Confederates. Thus, Southern democracy contributed to the laws against which Homer Plessy and the New Orleans Citizens' Committee sought to fight.

Re-Union

The price for readmission of the former confederate states was : (1) assent to the Constitution; (2) adoption of equal rights provisions in their respective state constitutions; and (3) ratification of the Thirteenth–Fifteenth Amendments. Unfortunately, due to an assassin's bullet, President Lincoln would not see the completion of this work. As the *Plessy* case would highlight, having these provisions alone, without the force and weight of federal law to enforce them, was insufficient to protect African Americans. This is one reason it was so easy for the South to recover from slavery's abolishment—and to implement Jim Crow.

Factual Background of *Plessy*

General Facts

The *Plessy* case actually began prior to Plessy's action to oppose the Separate Car Law. Albion W. Tourgée, the lawyer chosen to represent Homer Plessy, initially challenged Louisiana's Separate Car Law under the Commerce Clause of the US Constitution. In this initial challenge, Tourgée instructed Daniel Desdunes to travel from New Orleans to Mobile, Alabama, across state lines, and to attempt to travel in the car reserved for whites. Attorney Tourgée then argued that Louisiana's Separate Car or Accommodations Law was unconstitutional under the Commerce Clause, as it infringed upon Congress's power to regulate interstate commerce.

In order to understand this case, under the Commerce Clause (Article 1, Section 8 of the US Constitution), Congress may regulate commerce with foreign nations, with Native Americans, and among the several states (interstate commerce). Thus, if a state tried to regulate an activity in one of these areas, such laws would be preempted or overruled by Congress. Alternatively, the state would at least have to seek Congress's permission prior to regulating the activity. By having the initial test take place in interstate commerce, Attorney Tourgée sought to show that the Louisiana law attempted to regulate an activity falling under the purview of Congress, without Congressional approval, thus violating the Constitution.

Attorney Tourgée was successful, as the Louisiana Supreme Court ruled that the state's Separate Car Law applied only to intrastate travel or travel only within Louisiana.[8] Thus this law could not prevent Desdunes from riding in the railcar reserved for whites on his trip from Louisiana to Alabama.

In this way, Tourgée incrementally limited the reach of Jim Crow segregation at least for the moment. Following this initial test, he continued working with the Citizens' Committee. Seeking to illustrate the absurdity of the Louisiana Separate Car Law, Tourgée suggested that the test person, or plaintiff in this new case, should be someone who appeared to be white. He wanted to argue whiteness as a property right in an attempt to persuade the Justices of the US Supreme Court that the case was about property rather than race. This is one of the reasons that Homer Plessy, only one-eighth African by descent, was an ideal person to challenge the law. Tourgée's rationale was that if Plessy's mixed, non-discernible African blood was sufficient to remove him from being white, then state law had essentially created a distinction without a difference. As in all other categories, Plessy should be considered white and entitled to the privileges of whites, including being able to ride in any rail car. The foresight, or lack thereof, embodied in this argument will be discussed in the next chapter, particularly as this point would reverberate for the next half century.

Another reason for choosing Plessy was that he was considered to be a man of good moral character. Moreover, the East Louisiana Railroad Company, which owned the railcar in which Plessy chose to challenge the law, was complicit in the challenge.[9] This is because, if the law were upheld as valid, there would be additional costs for East Louisiana to have more railcars separating whites and blacks. To them, segregation was expensive. Therefore, they silently hoped that the law would be overturned and thus supported Plessy and the Citizens' Committee's efforts to that end. As indicated previously, on June 7, 1892, this country began to be changed forever, when Homer Plessy sat in the car reserved for whites on a trip from New Orleans to Covington, Louisiana.[10]

Case Timeline

Homer Plessy was tried before Judge John H. Ferguson, in Criminal District Court in Orleans Parish on October 28, 1892. As expected, Homer Plessy was ultimately convicted of violating the Separate Car Law.[11] The case did not arrive at the US Supreme Court until February 1893. However, the case was deliberately delayed at Tourgée's request for reasons to be discussed later. Thus, on or about April 13, 1896, the U.S. Supreme Court heard oral argument in the case.[12]

Lawyers

Unlike Dred and Harriett Scott in their case, Homer Plessy primarily had one lead attorney—Tourgée—for the duration of his case. This is likely because this case was an actual strategic challenge to segregation laws. Born in Ohio in 1838, Tourgée was a lot of "former" things: carpetbagger, Union soldier, radical Republican, judge, and author.[13] Attorney Tourgée has been described as the most vocal and militant white supporter and advocate for the rights of African Americans during the last two decades of the 1800s.[14]

After relocating to North Carolina, he helped to draft much of the Reconstruction portions of the Constitution for the Old North (as North Carolina was known), which was crucial to the state's readmission to the Union after the Civil War. Tourgée also authored a book—*A Fool's Errand*, about his time in the South during Reconstruction—that was published in 1879, after the period's end.[15] His background and history explain very clearly how Reconstruction bore on his arguments before the Supreme Court in *Plessy*. For instance, Tourgée successfully helped North Carolina's first female member of the state bar gain admission. In fact, it is this background that made him the preferred candidate of the Citizens' Committee to lead Plessy's legal team. The Committee's head, Louis A. Martinet, held many of the same ideals and theories as Tourgée regarding use of the law to challenge segregation and remove the vestiges of slavery following the Civil War.

In addition, Tourgée had a history of challenging laws from his time as an abolitionist in the North. Indeed, some of the legal theories he brought to bear can be traced back to his experiences seeking relief in Northern courts. The very novel theories he advanced for dismantling segregation did not always lead to success in his attempts to use the law to overturn the evils of the day; nevertheless, he was up to the task of representing Plessy, making a direct attack on the Louisiana Separate Car Law, and seeking to expand the protections of the Fourteenth Amendment for people of African descent.

By the time the Citizens' Committee contacted Tourgée, he had left the South, basically giving up on it, following the end of Reconstruction. He no doubt observed how much of what he fought for on the battlefield and in the courtroom was being eroded by Jim Crow laws, and how all he did for the cause of freedom and equality for formerly enslaved people was quickly proving to be a fool's errand—hence the title of his book. He was living in New York at the time and had not actually practiced law in six years. For this reason, in the event of procedural questions, Tourgée depended upon local counsel, James G. Walker.[16] Moreover, for the US Supreme Court appeal, he engaged former solicitor general and friend Samuel F. Phillips to assist and provide technical advice and support.[17] Meanwhile lawyers for the defense, the State of Louisiana, seeking to uphold the law, were Milton J. Cunningham, Louisiana Attorney General and Attorney Alexander P. Morse.[18]

Judges

Immediately prior to *Plessy*, the Supreme Court had undergone drastic changes, which is not that uncommon in the Court's history, in contrast to today, when it is the norm for Supreme Court Justices to serve for thirty years or more (the Court recently achieved the historic milestone of being the longest-serving Supreme Court in history). Historically, the Court did not have Justices who served several decades. In Plessy's case, Chief Justice Melville Fuller presided. The author of the majority opinion was Justice Henry Billings Brown. The author of the dissenting opinion was Justice John Marshall Harlan, Sr. These were the most notable Justices in the case, given their participation in it, although there were six others at the time of *Plessy*.[19] Prior to serving on the Court, Justice Brown's career and judicial service included serving for a period as the US District Judge for the Eastern District of Michigan.[20] Yet he was not considered the most illustrious justice on the Court at that time.

Chief Justice Fuller was a staunch conservative. Like many of the other Justices at that time, he did not support the federal government's intervention in slavery or in the South as it related to Reconstruction and enforcing civil and equal rights for African Americans. Thus, it was unlikely that Chief Justice Fuller would rule in Plessy's favor. That said, it is not clear why he did not write the majority opinion, as was the custom. Perhaps he did not want to go down in infamy like Chief Justice Taney in *Dred Scott*. Given that the opinion was supported by a seven-to-one decision, it is likely that the other Justices' judicial philosophy and ideology were very close to those of Chief Justice Fuller and Associate Justice Brown. This had also been made evident through their rulings in the area of civil rights prior to *Plessy*. Even Justice Harlan's background was at least similar to that of the other Justices, as was his view of African Americans as inferior persons. Thus, this Court was by no means sharply divided. Except for the ringing dissent of the Sr. Justice Harlan, the decision in *Plessy* would speak with one loud, almost singular voice.

Legal Arguments
Precedent

In terms of precedent, by the time *Plessy* reached the US Supreme Court, its result was a foregone conclusion. An anti–civil rights sentiment was already apparent in the Court, as it had begun to erode or limit the effectiveness of many of the civil rights laws and amendments passed by the Reconstruction Congress.

For instance, in the *Slaughterhouse Cases* (1873), mentioned above—which, like *Plessy*, originated in New Orleans—butchers in the area challenged a monopoly granted by the state to one meat-packing business in New Orleans. The Supreme Court decided narrowly and perhaps surprisingly that the Fourteenth Amendment only protected formerly enslaved persons, and since none of the butchers had been enslaved, they could not win the case.[21] Moreover, and perhaps even more damaging, the Court decided that the Fourteenth Amendment created state and national citizenship, and that merely providing a state contract to one business had no effect on the butchers' national citizenship.[22] Similarly, in *Munn v. Illinois*, decided in 1877, the Court decided that states can set maximum rates for grain storage, as this was a valid exercise of state police power (actions taken by the state to address the health, safety, and welfare of the state and its citizens).[23] The Court indicated that the case involved property in the public interest, which could then be regulated by the state. Further, in *Santa Clara v. Southern Pacific*, decided in 1886—ten years before *Plessy*—the Court held that Southern Pacific Railroad's rights under the Fourteenth Amendment were violated by Santa Clara in that the city taxed the railroad's fencing as an asset while it denied the railroad the ability to deduct the cost of a mortgage like a natural person could under state law.[24] In doing so, the Supreme Court established for the first time that corporations were protected by the Fourteenth Amendment. This was a major departure from the original intent of the law, and it was in direct contrast to the Court's previous decision in the *Slaughterhouse Cases*.

But while the Supreme Court proceeded to expand rights under the Fourteenth Amendment for everyone else, including corporations, it was eroding the protections and rights afforded formerly enslaved people. These cases began to lay out the Court's strong support of the broad authority of the several states and the limited authority of the federal government, a tension that was ultimately a factor in its decision in *Plessy*. This reversal by the Court begs the question of whether the Justices were simply restricting Congress' actions in an effort to curtail the federal government's power or whether they actually opposed the civil rights laws Congress had passed. The interesting thing about the latter position is that today, in choosing to limit the reach of many civil rights laws previously upheld—most notably, of course, the Voting Rights Act—the

Supreme Court seems to be engaged in a similar practice. Finally, in the case of *Hall v. DeCuir* decided in 1878, the Supreme Court held that the Equal Accommodations Act of 1869 only applied to in-state travel, and thus states were permitted to decide on their own whether to allow segregation between whites and blacks.[25]

Plessy's Arguments

Part of the rationale of the Citizens' Committee's choice to make a frontal assault on segregation was to force the US Supreme Court—this nation's highest legal authority and, in the words of Chief Justice John Marshall, the sole expositor of the Constitution—to reconcile segregation with the equal-protection commands of the Fourteenth Amendment. In fact, Tourgée's strategy was not to seek to overturn Homer Plessy's conviction but rather to protest against the State of Louisiana for forcing Plessy and others of African descent to ride in separate rail cars.[26] The merits of such a strategy were questionable (later generations of civil rights lawyers would certainly question them), but the arguments put forth for Plessy drew largely on the background and history of Tourgée and the Citizens' Committee. For instance, Tourgée cited the Supreme Court case of *Louisville, New Orleans, and Texas Railway Co. v. Mississippi*, decided in 1890, in which the Court reserved the power to rule on whether individuals could be compelled to use separate railcars.[27]

Also, Tourgée argued in his brief that the Fourteenth Amendment introduced the concept of national citizenship. Further, he argued that it was an affirmative statement of rights granted to citizens, including equal protection, due process, and privileges and immunities. This was in stark contrast to previous Supreme Court precedent, which viewed the amendment as a restriction on what the state could do toward citizens. As is obvious, the latter is a much narrower view of the Amendment, while the former is a broader and more expansive view. However, Tourgée argued that the *Plessy* case turned on the question of whether the Fourteenth Amendment restricted the "[right] of the state to label one citizen as white and another as colored..."[28] And Tourgée advanced another principle argument, that the Declaration of Independence was more than merely an ideological premise; it was a foundational document upon which the U.S. government was established and by which it should be bound. He reiterated the fundamental principles of a free republican government. Moreover, perhaps unadvisedly, he questioned the Supreme Court's recent jurisprudence on the Thirteenth and Fourteenth Amendments.

Some have argued that in doing so, Tourgée doomed his argument, and consequently *Plessy*, to failure.[29] But Tourgée and the Citizens' Committee were under no misconception, nor did they indulge in the rose-colored glasses view of the case. They knew that the case was a long shot, even without the Court's recent jurisprudence and given that Reconstruction had ended. Whether his arguments illustrated this or not, Tourgée appeared to have a keen understanding of the Supreme Court, especially in the area of civil rights. He remarked that "[t]he [C]ourt has always been the foe of liberty ... until forced to move by public opinion."[30] Thus he requested a delay of the Court's ruling, no doubt hoping that public opinion would sway more toward Plessy's direction. Tourgée's request for delay was granted, and up to three years elapsed between the filing of the appeal and the decision by the Court.[31]

Alas, despite Tourgée and the Citizens' Committee's highest hopes, due to various events, public opinion did not turn in their favor. These events included the loss of Frederick Douglass; the rise of lynchings; the apparent capitulation of Booker T. Washington—the unofficial leader of the African American population at that time—on the issue of racial inferiority; and Congressional repeal of many Reconstruction-era laws designed to assist African Americans with full realization of civil rights after the Civil War.[32]

Ferguson's Arguments in Plessy

Counsel for the State of Louisiana (although the case was in the name of Plessy) argued that under the 10th Amendment, and the state's police powers (laws designed to protect the health, safety, welfare, and to purportedly maintain order), Louisiana had the authority to enact the Separate Car Law.[33] Moreover, Louisiana argued that the law applied equally, as whites were prohibited from riding in the car reserved for negro people, and the state actually stipulated to the law's equality.[34] Accordingly, the attorneys for the defense in *Plessy* argued that the Louisiana Separate Car Law was constitutional in every sense.

Majority Opinion

Ultimately, on May 18, 1896, by a seven-to-one vote, the Court ruled against Plessy. The majority opinion was written by Justice Brown, joined by Chief Justice Fuller, along with Justices Field, Gray, Shiras, White, and Peckham.[35] Justice John Marshall Harlan Sr. authored the lone dissenting opinion in the case.[36] To support its ruling, the majority cited *Roberts v. City of Boston*, decided in 1849, stating that the Fourteenth Amendment "could not have been" enacted to get rid of color/race distinctions in the social, rather than the political, realm.[37] This rationale is very interesting in that the Court has used similar rationales to restrict or narrow the application of a congressionally enacted statute in later generations after *Plessy*. It is curious whether Congress ever actually said this anywhere or if the Court merely substituted its own view of the Fourteenth Amendment, especially given that the Court did not point to any identifiable legislative intent to justify this conclusion. The Court's rationale in *Plessy* emphasizes Tourgée's point about its being the foe of liberty, unwilling to extend protections to African Americans based on public or social policy. This is also consistent with the Court's jurisprudence immediately prior to *Plessy*. One by one, these cases illustrated the Court's view of the Fourteenth Amendment as a negative command to restrict the state from taking certain actions, rather than as a positive grant of rights to be enforced.

For instance, in the *Civil Rights Cases*, decided in 1883, the Court held that non-state actors may discriminate.[38] Following this rationale, however, it would seem that the opposite would be true for Plessy. In addition, of note, the Court indicated that Plessy's argument—that separate-but-equal labels the African American race with a badge of inferiority—was simply a fallacy that was only believed by or evident to them. This point is particularly interesting in that it appears that the Court is accusing Plessy of "playing the race card," to borrow from vernacular used in later times. This seems to be a flawed statement, as if somehow African Americans were responsible for placing themselves in slavery prior to Reconstruction, and after Reconstruction, African Americans were responsible for enacting laws that would restrict themselves from participating in various public activities with whites. It appears that Justice Harlan makes note of the circularity of this argument in his dissent. Furthermore, for the first time, the Supreme Court introduced the standard of reasonableness into the decision-making framework. Thus, the Court's majority continued, it could not conclude that the Louisiana Separate Car Law's requirement or permission to separate the races was per se unreasonable.[39] It was clear that the Court decided that equality could not be the product of legislation. This begs the question, in the Court's thinking: if equality cannot be produced in the courts or in the legislature, can it be produced through the law at all? The answer to this question will be discussed below.

Finally, the Court said that Plessy's Thirteenth Amendment argument was not sufficient to warrant discussion. The majority opinion indicated that it did not matter whether Plessy was white or colored, but that it was within the state's power to decide how individual races would be determined under their law—and that determination would control which railcar he could travel in, based on his race. Thus, while disappointing, the Court's decision was not a surprise.

There were no concurring opinions in *Plessy*, a noticeable difference from *Dred Scott*, among other differences between the cases which will be discussed in a later chapter. No, the lack of a concurrence underscores the prevailing view that most—including Tourgée and the Citizens' Committee—held, which was that the Court was pretty unified in its belief that separate-but-equal did not violate the Constitution. It also underscores a subtle, and perhaps often overlooked point, which is that at least in the minds eight of the nine Justices at the time, the decision in *Plessy* was not controversial. In the history of the Court, and even in today's time, where a case carries with it the ire of controversy or is such that it may create or receive national attention, the Justices may be inclined to offer separate concurring opinions to voice their analyses or positions that differ from the majority opinion. That did not happen here. This is unique particularly in contrast to other civil rights decisions, which would have tremendous impact on the nation—for instance, *Dred Scott*, in which every Justice issued either a separate concurrence or a dissenting opinion. Here, in a case that would remain the law and impact millions of African Americans across more than half a century, there would be little to no disagreement among most of the members of the highest court in the land. Separate but equal, then, would be a rainstorm that would have the ripple effects of an F5 tornado ripping up the landscape of equality for African Americans in the United States.

In the majority opinion itself, Justice Brown indicated that merely segregating the Negro race from whites, or creating a legal distinction that does so, does not violate the Fourteenth Amendment's equal protection provisions.[40] It thus concluded the opposite of what Congress intended when it enacted the Fourteenth Amendment. This is evidenced by the majority's citing of *Roberts v. City of Boston* (1849) to support its opinion. That case involved US Senator Charles Sumner, a principal architect and supporter of the Fourteenth Amendment, who argued unsuccessfully in that case that any racial segregation was a violation of the equality that Congress carved into the Fourteenth Amendment.[41] The irony of this result is that Sumner's failing argument helped motivate him to turn to legislation in order to achieve this end, and the Supreme Court in *Plessy* ultimately ended up siding with the Court in the *Roberts* case, against the very position that Sumner helped place in the Fourteenth Amendment itself. As such, the majority in *Plessy* in many ways substituted its own judgment for that of Congress—an act that many watchers and critics of the Court argue should never have been allowed to happen.

Dissent

Justice John Marshal Harlan, Sr., a Kentucky-born Justice issued what would become one of the most famous and often discussed dissenting opinions in the history of the Court. But Justice Harlan was an unlikely dissenter in this particular case, given his heritage and his opposition to secession, emancipation, and the Thirteenth and Fourteenth Amendments to the Constitution. Nevertheless, he would become the Court's most ardent defender of African American rights to that point in history.[42] His dissent pointed out that the majority opinion's assertion—that the Separate Car Law was focused on something other than the exclusion of African Americans from the railcars used by whites—was simply erroneous. Justice Harlan went even further to acknowledge that the veiled disguise of the equality of separate accommodations or facilities was not to be believed by anyone, and famously said that it wouldn't "atone for the wrong done this day" in *Plessy*.[43] Thus Justice Harlan appeared to adopt many themes from Tourgée's arguments. This is notable in that it helped to preserve Tourgée's arguments for future generations.

Justice John M. Harlan, Sr. Associate Justice U.S. Supreme Court, lone dissenter in Plessy v. Ferguson case-Courtesy Library of Congress

Perhaps the most famous and oft-quoted portion of Harlan's dissent is his assertion that the Constitution should be colorblind. However, what may not be widely known, is that he continued on to say that the white race was superior and would continue to be so. Justice Harlan's words prove that simply using the word colorblind does not automatically render its user as opposing racism or white supremacy. It is interesting that when quoting Justice Harlan's use of *colorblindness*, most—including members of the Court—do not include mention of the white-superiority sentiment. African Americans, then have a complicated relationship with Justice Harlan: on one hand, he agreed with Plessy's claim regarding the necessity of the removal of the badge of inferiority to achieve equality under the Fourteenth Amendment; but on the other hand, he—like the Justices in the majority—believed in the inferiority of African Americans to whites. This is not an unusual occurrence throughout African American history, particularly in the history of civil rights legislation, when prominent whites have provided support for the equal rights of African Americans in principle, but not in substance.

However, misguided on race Justice Harlan may have been, he was still bold enough to write a dissenting opinion, and insofar as equality is addressed in the law, he ended up on the right side of history even if he took the wrong road to get there. Carrying forward more of Tourgée's argument, Justice Harlan indicated his belief that not only did the Reconstruction Congress desire the outcome of freedom through equality under the Fourteenth Amendment, it also desired liberty in the freedom to move or travel from place to place in the United States without restriction. It was not lost on Justice Harlan that Plessy's ability to travel from New Orleans to Covington, or Daniel Desdunes's freedom to travel from New Orleans to Mobile, Alabama, was at stake in this case and was implicated by the Fourteenth Amendment.

For if one is not able to travel freely, openly, without restriction or restraint, then one cannot be said to truly be free from the bonds of slavery. Indeed, Justice Harlan was likely thinking about the many laws and codes that existed during slavery, prohibiting enslaved people from being able to travel to various places without escort or proper documentation. He likely saw the restriction of Plessy's movement as similar to a situation in which Plessy was in bonds and needed some slaveholder's documentation or seal in order to travel to another place. It is of note that Justice Harlan acknowledged that, contrary to recent precedent by the US Supreme Court prior to *Plessy*, the Fourteenth Amendment was drafted primarily for African Americans. It likely seemed illogical to him that the people for whom the Fourteenth Amendment was drafted were now being told that its application was limited toward them. Especially, while at the same time the Court was expanding the Fourteenth Amendment's application to others, including corporations. Thus, Justice Harlan contended, much like Justice Curtis' dissent in *Dred Scott*, that the majority's opinion was antithetical to both the spirit and letter of the US Constitution.

Despite Justice Harlan's strong words, the majority opinion, for most, was merely confirmation of what had already become accepted practice by that time: segregation of whites and blacks. Though it was not accepted by all, including Tourgée, Plessy, the Citizens' Committee, and others like them, the decision in *Plessy*, was accepted by the majority of the population and, at that time, by all three branches of the federal government, the president, the Supreme Court, and Congress. Justice Harlan was keenly aware of the US Supreme Court's march away from the Fourteenth Amendment's original intent, as was evident in its previous rulings.

Nevertheless, almost half a century later, Justice Harlan's dissent and to some extent Tourgée's arguments, would win the day. In fact,

Justice Harlan's dissent is an example of how sometimes years later, a dissenting opinion can be remembered more than the majority opinion. It also provides evidence of how in the life of the Court, the dissenting opinion at one point in history can eventually become the majority opinion at a different point in history. For African Americans, however, the wait for Justice Harlan's and Tourgée's view of the Thirteenth, Fourteenth, and Fifteenth Amendments to prevail, would be long and painful.

──── CHAPTER 6 ────

FAIL UP: THE OUTCOMES OF PLESSY

Immediate Impact of Plessy

Business as Usual

As if it were a foregone conclusion, the decision by the US Supreme Court in *Plessy v. Ferguson* was issued without much fanfare at all. In fact, the case received very little mainstream national attention, and there was little to no national movement or discussion to end Jim Crow. Three other decisions announced on the same day as *Plessy* all received greater news coverage.[1] The *New York Times*, for example, included the *Plessy* decision on page three in its section discussing railway news;[2] neither the *Boston Globe* nor the *Chicago Daily Tribune* reported the decision;[3] and the *Hartford Courier* gave it merely two paragraphs.[4] What is most startling about the news reporting on *Plessy* is that most of these newspapers generally provided significant coverage of Supreme Court cases, yet what was probably the most important case of the century barely received an honorable mention.

Those news outlets that were obvious supporters of segregation, on the other hand, had a great deal to say in support of the decision. For instance, the *New Orleans Daily Picayune*, echoing the voice of segregationists, lauded the decision and predicted that it would lead to the enforcement of separate-car laws throughout the South.[5] The newspaper compared the bringing of the *Plessy* case to socialism, calling it an attempt to subvert individual rights and anathema to democracy.[6] The *New Orleans Times Democrat* lauded the original decision of Judge Ferguson, finding no constitutional violation and asserting that African Americans should not stand side-by-side with whites.[7] And the *Richmond Virginia Dispatch* hailed the decision, offering a further opinion on the value of separation as a buffer between African Americans—whom it described as not well behaved—and whites.[8] Although the *Boston Globe* did not report on the case, it did report on the Boston Colored League's statement condemning the result in the case.[9] The *Atlanta Journal Constitution* reported on the case in its section covering blacks and whites.[10] And the Democratic Populist Party made no mention of the case. Thus, despite the huge impact of *Plessy* on the nation and especially on African Americans, it was met with very little press attention nationally.

As usual, many in favor of segregation and white supremacy went through intellectual gymnastics to arrive at any possible justification for segregation of whites from African Americans. Unfortunately, this kind of rationalization of white supremacy would permeate even into the legal scholarship. The *Virginia Law Register* responded that the decision in *Plessy* followed what it called Natural Law.[11] Unfortunately, attitudes like this would continue after *Plessy*, into the 1900s, through the civil rights movement, and even up to this day, although in a somewhat subtler context.

Nevertheless, there were news outlets on the side of abolition and anti-segregation that reported on the case. For instance, the black and Roman Catholic presses displayed anger and fear that in not stopping laws that enforced segregation, the Supreme Court's decision in *Plessy* sanctioned segregation.[12] The *Rochester Democrat and Chronicle* praised Justice Harlan's ringing dissent and condemned the majority for its decision.[13] The newspaper also accurately predicted that after *Plessy* other southern legislatures would follow Louisiana's lead and pass similar laws designed to restrict the rights of African Americans.[14] More directly, the *Donahue Magazine* remarked that after the *Plessy* decision, if state legislatures were able to pass such segregationist laws, it was as if *Dred Scott* had not been decided, nor the Civil War fought, declaring that racial selfishness would be the curse and danger of this country.[15] And from a legal perspective, the *American Law Review* predicted rather presciently that eventually Justice Harlan's dissenting view would become the majority rule of the day.[16]

A Drop in the Bucket

Perhaps Tourgée and the New Orleans Citizens' Committee's strategy of using Homer Plessy, who was only one-eighth black, as a plaintiff forced the Supreme Court and even state legislatures to conclude that it was not possible to determine someone's race only by looking at them. Even the Supreme Court's decision, while it upheld the constitutionality of Louisiana's Separate Car Law, did not determine that Plessy was indeed black. Instead, it allowed the state to come up with a means for determining whether Plessy was black and prohibited from riding in the railcar with whites. As a result, in order to more fully implement *Plessy*, Louisiana and other states had to devise mechanisms for distinguishing African Americans from whites.

Albion W. Tourgée Lead Attorney for Homer Plessy
- Courtesy of State Archives of North Carolina

Louisiana began this process during the trial of the case, when the state's assistant district attorney argued that it was reasonable for whites not to have to ride in the car with blacks given their foul odor.[17] Following this kind of logic, southern states began to make mixed-race marriages illegal and created descriptions of the characteristics that would determine who was considered "black."[18] In doing so, the states and society at large began to socially construct the meaning of race in this country. By the mid-1920s, Virginia adopted the one-drop rule, relying on genealogical background and using the history of an individuals' fathers, mothers, and even great-grandparents to determine racial identification.[19] Of course other states would follow suit, and the one-drop rule would become the racial standard in this country for almost the next half-century.

Strange Fruit

One of the more gruesome consequences of *Plessy*'s decision was the rise in lynchings across this country. While lynchings had been on the rise during the time between *Plessy*'s filing and the decision, the Supreme Court's confirmation of segregation in its decision only served to embolden those who would use violence and fear to maintain segregation at all costs, leading to lynchings of African Americans. It is not clear whether the Supreme Court ever considered the wide-ranging effects of its decision, and whether lynchings were even on the Court's radar at the time *Plessy* was decided. The Court was certainly aware of the activities of groups like the Ku Klux Klan. During its march toward *Plessy*, the Court began to roll back many legal protections enacted by the Reconstruction Congress, including cases involving criminalizing the activities of the Ku Klux Klan. Thus at least on some level the Court was either deliberately indifferent or recklessly disregarded the impact *Plessy* might have on violence toward African Americans, including lynchings, by the Ku Klux Klan and other groups. Lynching became one of the main tools in suppressing African American resistance not only in the South but in other parts of the country as well.

Not only did the decision in *Plessy* contribute to the increase in these violent terrorist acts,[20] it also made it more difficult to protect African Americans from these acts. And Congress dragged its heels: for decades, antilynching legislation was proposed, but only recently has such legislation been moved closer toward enactment into law. Furthermore, the National Memorial for Peace and Justice, which opened in 2018 in Montgomery, Alabama, is devoted almost exclusively to the history of lynching in this country. Lynching is among the ugliest parts of the African American experience—and of the history of the United States. *Plessy*'s result gave those who were already inclined to commit such acts the confidence to do so to an even greater extent.

"Pontius" Supreme Court

The Supreme Court's decision in *Plessy* was part of a larger development that began shortly after Lincoln's assassination. With the appointment of new justices, the Court began to move away from the wishes of the Reconstruction Congress. Not unlike its leanings in the first decades of the twenty-first century, slowly but surely, the Court got out of the business of protecting the rights of African Americans following the end of slavery and the Civil War. In addition, and perhaps more damaging, the Court began to curtail the ability of the other branches of the federal government to do so. It voided the Civil Rights Act of 1875, and in opinion after opinion either outright invalidated Congressional acts or narrowly interpreted constitutional amendments to accomplish this result. Thanks to the Hayes-Tilden Compromise of 1877 (discussed in chapter 4) not only did African Americans no longer have a political ally in the White House, they also no longer had the support of Congress. More importantly, there were no longer federal troops in the South to prevent the insurgents of the former Confederacy from rising up and crushing the glimmer of freedom that African Americans briefly enjoyed after the Civil War. Just as Congress abandoned military enforcement of African American civil rights, the Supreme Court eroded or severely limited legal enforcement of those rights.

As history would illustrate, at the turn of the twentieth century many of the Justices of the Supreme Court just did not believe in the federal government's authority or purpose in maintaining the post-slavery freedom and equality of African Americans. Many of the Justices publicly stated their views to this effect.[21] By doing so, similar to the biblical account of the Roman leader Pontius Pilatus washing his hands of the trial, condemnation, and crucifixion of Jesus Christ, the Court proverbially "washed it hands" of Reconstruction. Thus, the Reconstruction Congress's constitutional amendments and federal laws—which were clearly directed toward liberating African Americans not only from slavery but from the remaining vestiges that would prevent them from enjoying the full benefits of citizenship—would not be enforced. If the purpose of the Supreme Court encompasses giving effect to Congressional actions, when it fails to do so, how then does it fulfill its purpose, and what is its value? It was clear during this period in the Court's history that it believed its purpose excluded standing in the way of the spread of segregation throughout the states. Therefore, *Plessy* remains the hallmark of this period in the Court's history.

Economic Impact of *Plessy*
Slavery by Another Name

Plessy not only had grave physical impacts on the lives of African Americans, it also had a tremendous economic impact. The post-*Plessy* landscape had African Americans fighting among themselves for their share of equality. This included black labor unions.[22] By the end of the nineteenth century, African Americans began to model white behavior, in terms of economic and political standing.[23]

And whites continued to look at blacks through the eyes of segregation, with segregated housing, facilities, and accommodations. Thus arose the view of the black side of town as "dirty and dingy, a negative stereotype that has continued down through history."[24] The *Plessy* decision helped to perpetuate the narrative that African Americans were indeed inferior in every way, not just intellectually or socially but economically as well. *Plessy* ensured not only that African Americans were separated from whites but that by law, states could make certain they remained that way. Further, the case guaranteed that the opportunities, benefits, and protections for whites and African Americans were anything but equal. The Supreme Court had previously struck down the Civil Rights Act of 1875, which provided for equality in accommodations, transportation, and other areas, and *Plessy* compounded this decision by declaring it reasonable for states to deliberately create inequality between African Americans and whites.

Costs of Separate but Equal

Perhaps one of the silver linings of the strategy by the Citizens' Committee and Tourgée was the enlistment of help from the East Louisiana Railroad Company (the railroad company whose car Plessy sat on to challenge the law) in the case.[25] The railroad company's position in the case was a clever maneuver not only from the standpoint of the testing strategy but also in the attempt to make an economic argument in the case. Despite Tourgée's view that the Court was very concerned about property rights, it does not appear that the Court valued the economic portion of the case in any meaningful way. This is an important practical, if not legal, point. Throughout its history the Court has decided cases based heavily on the economic or business impact. In many cases, the Court has sided with or ruled in favor of economic interests. Yet its decision in *Plessy* probably had a large negative economic impact on businesses at that time.

Having separate cars for whites and African Americans would require additional cars, which would mean additional costs for the railroad company. The same logic applies in other areas, education for instance, where separate schools would require additional facilities and more funding. In restaurants and other places of public accommodations, separate water fountains and separate restrooms would require additional costs. These costs would continue over the next sixty years. The only reason or purpose for these additional costs to states and businesses in all of these areas was that African Americans and whites should be separated, period. This was the least practical result of the Supreme Court's decision in *Plessy*. For example, from a legal education standpoint, *Plessy* would require the State of North Carolina to create a separate law school, North Carolina Central University, for African Americans.[26] Additionally, *Plessy* required the state of Alabama to split the difference between in-state tuition and the cost of tuition for African American students to attend law schools outside Alabama. All of these costs and many more are directly attributable to the decision in *Plessy*. Ironically, this would also lead to *Plessy*'s undoing. Perhaps this is an indication of Tourgée's genius, which will be discussed in a later chapter.

Legal Impact of Plessy
On the Supreme Court

Justice Harlan's dissent, which probably received as much attention as the majority opinion, or more, voiced what many on the side of equality for African Americans already knew: the majority's opinion was openly hostile toward formerly enslaved people of African descent and sensitive to whites. This is true even though

Justice Harlan himself felt that African Americans were indeed inferior as the majority had intimated.[27] In his reflections on Justice Harlan's dissent years after *Plessy*, Justice Brown admitted that the Louisiana statute in the case was designed to keep African Americans and whites separate and to maintain a badge of servitude on the formerly enslaved people.[28] This directly refutes his assertion in the majority opinion, that the very same argument made by Tourgée was fiction and only thought of in the minds of the Plessy and other African-Americans.[29]

Thus, the Court's opinion in *Plessy* was not derived from anything other than segregationist thought and principles. The authors of the majority and dissenting opinions were in agreement on these principles. These facts, along with the other consequences of the decision in *Plessy*, helped to further darken the Court's stature in the minds of African Americans, as much as previous decisions of the Court had done. Indeed, it would take almost half of a century for the Court to overturn *Plessy*, but it is not clear whether the Court has, or will ever, overcome its historical effect on the Court or this country.

A Gathering of Black Codes

The attempt to overturn the Separate Car Law in Louisiana, like that in *Plessy*, was part of a larger overall strategy. As such, more than twenty-five boycotts of streetcars were carried out between the 1890s and the early 1900s.[30] Most were unsuccessful, although some were temporarily successful. With the hope that the Civil War Amendments would be interpreted on the side of freedom and equality, many cases were litigated at the US Supreme Court, thus creating a narrative of segregation by whites and resistance by African Americans. Nevertheless, from 1898—two years following *Plessy*—until 1910, South Carolina, North Carolina, Virginia, Maryland, and Oklahoma, keeping almost in lockstep with the

Confederacy, all passed separate-but-equal railcar and other laws segregating African Americans from whites.[31]

States' Rights

Since this country's founding, the idea of federalism has been a struggle for lawmakers, citizens, and judges alike. From early decisions of the US Supreme Court—including by perhaps its most well-known early presiding member, Chief Justice John Marshall—until the time of the *Plessy* case, questions persisted about the appropriate balance between the powers of the individual states and those of the federal government. Former Chief Justice John Marshall believed it was important to affirm the power of the federal government in the event of a conflict with the states.[32] Accordingly, he favored the supremacy of federal law over state law in these instances. However, his successors—Chief Justice Taney during the *Dred Scott* case and, later, Chief Justice Fuller at the time of *Plessy*—did not share this view. Instead, they had a narrower view of the federal government's power and a correspondingly broader view of states' rights, particularly when it came to issues of slavery and segregation. As a result, *Plessy*, like *Dred Scott*, was an extension of the latter rather than the former view of federalism.

Legalized Segregation

At the time, *Plessy* was really just a confirmation of the past two decades of Supreme Court jurisprudence in the area of civil rights. All of *Plessy*'s ancestry in the Court—including *DeCuir* and the *Civil Rights Cases*—actually could have been decided in a different way.[33] But as history records, they were decided against civil rights and freedom for African Americans, and in favor of segregationist state laws and Jim Crow. Thus, *Plessy* was almost a foregone conclusion when it arrived at the Supreme Court, which is evidenced by the fact that the ruling was not treated as remarkable.³⁴ This period of decisions may be properly characterized as the Jim Crow Supreme Court, given its impact and the fact that these decisions, of which *Plessy* was the capstone, explicitly and implicitly ushered in the era of segregation throughout the United States. Even the author of the majority opinion in *Plessy*, Justice Henry Billings Brown, remarked later, in 1903, that in hindsight, he was at least aware that their decisions resulted in possible injustice for African Americans.³⁵ Furthermore, as touched on above, the Supreme Court was indifferent to the lynchings, beatings, false convictions, and uses of derogatory comments like *Nigger* toward African Americans during this period.³⁶ The Supreme Court was at least a willing participant in the oppression of African Americans through its actions, and particularly through its inactions. Justice Brown further remarked that *Plessy* was a return to a strict constructionist philosophy of the Court that it later abandoned.

Impact of Plessy on the Civil Rights Movement
Defeated but Not Deterred

Despite the result in *Plessy*, African Americans continued to use litigation as a means of resistance to oppression and segregation.³⁷ After *Plessy* at least seventy-one cases were brought challenging segregation.³⁸ Furthermore, the NAACP, believed litigation to be its best option for progress. Charles Hamilton Houston, the original architect of the strategy to overturn *Plessy*, indeed saw litigation as a valid and viable tool for effecting social change. It is here that Houston recognized that Tourgée and the Citizens' Committee's attempt in *Plessy* was the right strategy, just possibly the wrong legal argument. In fact, in their defeat he would find the solution for many cases to come—cases that would desegregate institutions—before finally overturning *Plessy*. But it was not only on the legal front that civil rights leaders were not deterred. It is no small matter that the NAACP was formed a little over a decade after the *Plessy* decision. The Citizens' Committee was indeed an example for the NAACP to follow. The citizens coming together, getting organized, developing an agenda, formulating strategies both legal and otherwise, were all approaches that the NAACP and future civil rights organizations would use to advance their cause. Thus, even though they were not ultimately successful in *Plessy*, the Citizens' Committee offered proof for future generations of what could happen when a group of concerned African Americans refused to stand idly by and allow segregation to take hold of themselves or their people. Instead, they acted. In this way, the Citizens' Committee continued to live on through future organizations and civil rights leaders who would engage in litigation, mass protests, sit-ins, boycotts, and many other forms of civil disobedience to bring about change.

Bearing Witness

In the aftermath of *Plessy*, statistician Frederick L. Hoffman concluded that segregation was necessary to save African Americans and help them improve their morality.[39] Other African American civil rights leaders also weighed in on the *Plessy* decision. For instance, Booker T. Washington, who at that time was considered the unofficial leader of African Americans, commented that *Plessy* was not common sense, even if it might have been good law, which is questionable, as discussed in an earlier chapter. Washington went on to assert that while "colored" people contended that the accommodations were not equal despite charging the same price, they did not complain about the separation (or segregation).[40] Another prominent African American leader, Dr. W. E. B. DuBois, would come onto the scene after *Plessy*. He would go on to help found the Niagara Movement, which would eventually form the NAACP. In addition, novelist Charles W. Chestnut, with the *Boston Evening Transcript*, recounted reactions of African Americans to separate-car regulations and wrote *The Marrow of Tradition*, published in 1901, and *The Courts and the Negro*, published in 1908.[41]

A Path Forward

Roots of Promise

Despite the defeat in *Plessy*, Houston used the case to motivate African American lawyers to change it—including the lawyer who would lead the legal team that would argue *Brown v. Board of Education*, overturning *Plessy*.[42] Thus by stirring revolt in the Negro population, a result of the unfavorable litigation, *Plessy*'s decision did the opposite of what it was likely intended to do, at least in part. The NAACP began to see the courts almost as Tourgée and the Citizens' Committee had seen them: a means to stir action and encourage resistance.

More directly, *Plessy* was a learning tool for Houston and Thurgood Marshall as they began to seek to dismantle what *Plessy* had built. This is because Tourgée's strategy, though well-intentioned, was doomed to fail. Specifically, Houston and Marshall chose to attack various aspects of segregation rather than adopt the direct frontal assault employed by Tourgée and the Citizens' Committee in *Plessy*. Moreover, although Tourgée's brief and arguments sounded with poetry—which is not surprising given that he was an author and had written extensively—Houston and Marshall attempted in *Brown I* to develop a more practical strategy to dismantle segregation.

Nevertheless, their strategy did have some roots in Tourgée's arguments, and those arguments cannot be dismissed as a complete failure. Tourgée's arguments tied the Thirteenth, Fourteenth, and Fifteenth Amendments to slavery. Over half a century later, Marshall, in his argument before the US Supreme Court in *Brown*, made a similar point to the Justices. Marshall too made the case that the only purpose of segregated schools was to keep the formerly enslaved people of African descent, as near to their past enslaved condition as possible. Luckily for Marshall, fifty years was enough time for the Court and society to finally agree.

More broadly, *Plessy* reflects a common aspect of decisions of the US Supreme Court: sometimes losing litigation at one point in the Court's history reflects a community's legal vision; and at another point, litigation reflects a community's resolve to change the vision of the overall society to adopt that reflected by the previous losing side. That most certainly played a role in post-*Plessy* history and is an important part of its legacy as well.

A Legacy of Hope

Although *Plessy*'s result was expected and even anticipated by Tourgée and the Citizens' Committee, it still dealt a blow to all those on the side of civil rights for African Americans. It came at a very difficult time for African Americans. Perhaps the most influential and greatest champion for abolition and equal rights, Frederick Douglass, had passed on. Lynchings had become an important tool of the Ku Klux Klan and others. With the decision in the *Civil Rights Cases* invalidating the Civil Rights Act of 1875, African Americans had already lost an important piece of legislation aimed to provide greater equality. With the Hayes-Tilden Compromise of 1877, federal troops were removed from the South and from their role in enforcing the Civil War Amendments and other federal legislation. Then comes *Plessy*, near the turn of the century, to close the chapter on the nineteenth century almost as it began for African Americans:

with African Americans in an inferior position and stature in the eyes of the law.

Since being brought to the United States, African Americans as a people had been prisoners of hope. Given the successes of Reconstruction, however, it is likely that although this was a dark period that would last for more than half a century, it was also a time of great promise. This is seen through the early writers and figures who would come onto the scene, like Dr. DuBois, who would later write that the problem of the twentieth century would become that of the color line. In addition, Booker T. Washington would continue to build his school that would educate young African American minds and turn this school into a university that still stands to this day. The turn of the century would bring with it all the possibility of the new century. *Plessy* was the previous century, a century that included slavery and one of the bloodiest wars in history.

Thus, it is fortuitous that *Plessy* was decided on the foregone side of the century divide. It is likely that many African Americans realized that they could not wait until the federal government once again comes to their aid in protecting their rights and preserving equality for them. Instead, they would have to prepare themselves for the future and build up their own communities and institutions, to help take them into the new twentieth century. Within a few decades of *Plessy*, the Harlem Renaissance would usher in a new African American arts movement to encourage, uplift, and give voice and power to the pain and struggle of African Americans. Thus despite the failure in *Plessy*, the winds of change were a-blowin' toward a new era.

Leading to Its Own Demise

Whether or not it was clear to Tourgée and the Citizens' Committee at the time of *Plessy*, the decision itself, although steeped in white supremacy and segregation, provided the critical component for the strategy that would lead to its own end. First, on a more practical level, the requirement that African Americans attend schools that were their own essentially required that the best and brightest of African Americans would work together and learn together. Moreover, it resulted in African American teachers, professors, and scholars educating young African American minds, which greatly influenced students to excel in their endeavors. Indeed, as a byproduct of *Plessy*, state schools were developed for (at that time) Negroes that would become bastions of higher education. Historically Black Colleges and Universities (HCBUs) thrived during this period of segregation. They produced generations of some of the greatest leaders this country has ever seen, including Dr. Martin Luther King Jr. and Thurgood Marshall, a main architect in the *Brown* victory overturning *Plessy* who went on to become the first black Supreme Court Justice. The difficulties attendant to educational segregation can certainly be argued, and Justice Marshall remarked on his difficulties in having to attend Howard University Law School rather than the University of Maryland Law School. These difficulties became more of an inspiration for Marshall, and that inspiration began to develop the seed of change and growth that would eventually inspire him to challenge and knock down elements of separate-but-equal, culminating in the *Brown* decision.

This phenomenon of the most talented African American scholars descending on African American institutions of higher education is nowhere more prominent than at Howard Law School. Dean Charles Hamilton Houston, Harvard Law School educated, is the dean who would teach, mentor, and eventually work with Marshall to help dismantle segregation in this country. If Marshall had been able to attend the University of Maryland Law School, it is likely that he would never have encountered Dean Houston, but at

Howard, he did. It was Dean Houston who saw an opportunity with *Plessy* to train and teach young African American law students and then attorneys to fight against its mandate of separate-but-equal. Booker T. Washington and Dr. George Washington Carver produced similar results at Tuskegee Institute, now Tuskegee University. Mary McCleod Bethune founded Bethune-Cookman College, and there are countless other examples of HBCUs, where the fact that segregated colleges and universities were required allowed African American students to receive instruction from some of the giants of the African American academy. Thus, not only did *Plessy* produce African American scholars, lawyers, and other professionals who would thrive, it spurred a desire within African Americans that even if the law would not consider them equal to whites, they would strive to prove that they could meet and exceed the performance of whites in many areas. This spirit within African Americans was only increased and fueled by *Plessy*. Its mandate of segregation meant that African Americans were forced to help one another succeed, to grow families, businesses, schools, and other important institutions that would sustain and support their communities.

Plessy also did something else, by way of the rejection of the premise of the case: African Americans were challenged by *Plessy* not to take on the inferiority with which the decision attempted to brand them, but to do the contrary. African Americans—through the pain of slavery, after *Plessy*, and with the influence of Jim Crow segregation—were forced to maintain and create their dignity step by step, in a stark protest of *Plessy*'s edict. Whether explicit or not, the idea behind the decision was based in a belief that African Americans needed to be separated from whites, or vice versa, based on whites' superiority to African Americans. But African Americans rejected this notion and instead persevered to prove *Plessy* wrong.

Plessy not only provided the means of its own demise from a practical standpoint for African Americans, it also provided the legal basis for overturning the decision. One of the lessons that Houston and Marshall learned from Tourgée and the Citizens' Committee was that direct assaults do not work. Thus, rather than take the matter directly to the Supreme Court only to be defeated resoundingly, Houston and Marshall decided to make strategic challenges to segregation by attacking various facets of it. Moreover, one of the key strategies started by Houston and carried forward by Marshall was to prove that the separate facilities of educational institutions and other aspects of society were not in fact equal for African Americans. Houston and Marshall believed that if they could show that the separate facilities for African Americans were not even remotely similar in condition or quality to the facilities for whites, then the Court would be forced to order the states to make them equal or to desegregate them in order to comply with the mandate of the Fourteenth Amendment. Thus, Houston and Marshall used *Plessy* against itself to overturn it.

It was of course a brilliant strategy, and one that would provide a subtle assault on segregation, ultimately dismantling it. *Plessy* was merely a platitude offered by the states and accepted by the Supreme Court as a means of preserving segregation. It is doubtful that state leadership who fought so hard to preserve segregation intended or believed that the separate accommodations, educational institutions, and other facilities were or ever would be equal. This was a fatal flaw in their argument, seized upon by Houston and Marshall in their attack.

Houston and Marshall were able to piggyback upon some of Justice Harlan's points in his dissenting opinion—specifically, that the majority opinion's reasoning was flawed and suspect from its inception. The majority opinion merely perpetuated white supremacy, but it couched its reasoning in states' rights and reasonableness, when neither actually had anything to do with the essence of the case. This position is further supported by the majority opinion's ignoring the Reconstruction Congress's intent in adopting the Thirteenth, Fourteenth, and Fifteenth Amendments and substituting their own judgment for what these amendments should stand for. The majority opinion was replete with references to the Fourteenth Amendment, claiming that it could not change the nature of social interactions among blacks and whites. To the credit of Tourgée and the Citizens' Committee, their view of the Reconstruction Congress's intent was likely closer to and more accurate than the Supreme Court's view in *Plessy*. This obvious failure by the Court in *Plessy* is further exacerbated by the calls of Justices for judicial conservatism and strict constructionist philosophy, which were purported to have been undertaken by the Court. This is clearly a miscalculation given the fact that if the Court were being strict and conservative in its view of the Fourteenth Amendment, it would have decided *Plessy* differently, turning to what Congress intended in enacting the Civil War Amendments and similar laws designed to implement them. Instead, under the auspices of deciding law and expositing on the Constitution, the Court merely substituted its own opinions about the limitations on federal power to protect African Americans.

Plessy in Comparison

Plessy was indeed a huge setback to the cause of equality and freedom for African Americans, perhaps the most damaging Supreme Court decision in its history. This is not only because of its holding, but because of what others were able to do as a result of its holding. It is likely that Jim Crow segregation would not have survived had the case been decided differently.

Plessy represented a reversal of fortune for African Americans in this country. While there may not have been another case as detrimental to the long-term struggle, there have been some that have reversed the course for African Americans in in a significant way following *Plessy*. A good example is *Brown v. Board of Education of Topeka Kansas II*. After *Brown I* overturned *Plessy*'s principle, *Brown II* did as much as anything else to curtail the effect and implementation of *Brown I*. By declaring that public schools only had to desegregate with "all deliberate speed," the Supreme Court in *Brown II* gave license to local schoolboards, especially in the South, to use many subversive tactics to prevent, delay, and obstruct implementation of *Brown I*. Much like its predecessor Court in *Plessy*, the Court in *Brown II* gave license to southern and northern states to continue to implement segregation throughout this country. *Brown II* permitted school segregation to persist by bringing to a halt attempts at desegregation.

Further, in recognition of the visceral history of segregation and discrimination allowed by *Plessy*, *Regents of the University of California v. Bakke*, decided in 1978, erected a significant impediment for colleges and universities wishing to achieve a more diverse student body through the establishment of affirmative action programs in higher education. Additionally, in the area of government contracting, *Adarand Constructors, Inc. v. Pena* (1995) and *City of Richmond v. J.A. Croson* (1989), in almost mercurial fashion, used the equal-protection clause—the very same one that *Plessy* refused to interpret as preventing discrimination against African Americans—to strike down racial preferences in favor of African Americans in contracting. Thus, the same Supreme Court tribunal that refused to enforce the Fourteenth Amendment to protect African Americans from discrimination, had no problem enforcing it to protect whites from discrimination. It is examples like these that sow the seed of doubt about the Court's role in advancing racial equality in this country.

While *Plessy* may stand at the top of the mountain, it is not alone as an example of the US Supreme Court's, and by extension the federal government's, unwillingness to provide for equality for African Americans, even when it would provide it for whites and even nonhumans, such as corporations. *Plessy* did not exist in isolation, nor was it the last time that the Supreme Court would diminish and even destroy the rights of African Americans seeking full recognition of their citizenship under the law that was promised by the Thirteenth, Fourteenth, and Fifteenth Amendments. Nevertheless, *Plessy* still serves as a stark reminder of how fragile every measure of equality can be, and of the necessity to continue to preserve and protect such equality for future generations.

CHAPTER 7

AN EDUCATION: THE ROAD TO BROWN

Early Life of Oliver Brown

Much like Homer Plessy, Rev. Oliver Leo Brown, was recruited into history. But also, like Homer Plessy, he was not an unwilling participant. Like Homer Plessy's sitting on the segregated railcar was part of the plan of the Citizens' Committee, Rev. Oliver Brown's attempt to enroll his third grader and oldest daughter, Linda, in the all-white Sumner Elementary was part of a plan, by NAACP lawyers to challenge school segregation. Homer Plessy's staged action happened on a train, but Rev. Brown's staged action took place in a school. It was no surprise that he was not allowed to enroll his daughter. Like many African American husbands and fathers, Rev. Oliver Brown's life was a balancing-act between providing for his family and navigating the world of Jim Crow. Nevertheless, Rev. Oliver Brown did provide a life for his family in a somewhat integrated neighborhood. In addition to working as a boxcar welder for the Atchison, Topeka, and Santa Fe Railroad, Rev. Brown was later ordained as a minister in the African Methodist Episcopal (A.M.E.)

Church. In 1950, he served as an assistant pastor at the church he and his family attended.[1] But Rev. Brown was perplexed by more than just segregation in public accommodations, and other areas of society. He and Leola, his wife, were apprehended by the fact that their oldest daughter, Linda, had to attend the segregated Monroe elementary school many blocks away. This despite, Sumner Elementary School was only seven blocks from their house.[2] Moreover, when their other daughters were ready to go to elementary school, they would have to make the same trek, for one reason and one reason only: they were not white.

~Sumner Elementary School Topeka, Kansas-
Courtesy of the University of Kansas~

Rev. Brown's oldest daughter Linda played with other white kids in the neighborhood and they would have the best time with one another. There were no signs, partitions, or other obstructions to them playing with one another. But, when the time came to go to school, they would have to separate because of race. This was clearly an injustice in this scenario. What was Oliver Brown to do? Even before *Plessy* was decided and immediately after the end of Reconstruction, this is the way of life in the country. Despite the early efforts of the Reconstruction Congress to dismantle segregation in all its forms, including in public education, many states re-segregated virtually every area of society between blacks and whites. What is more, these states did so, with the blessing of the Congress and the President. Then in *Plessy v. Ferguson*, the Supreme Court essentially gave segregation the full force and effect of law. Although the U.S. Supreme Court did not hear a school desegregation case at the time of *Plessy*, based on the multitude of its other decisions, as *Plessy* proved, if it had, the Court would have allowed segregated public schools to continue. Thus, Rev. Brown was recruited to join twelve other families who worked with the NAACP in seeking to desegregate public schools in Topeka Kansas, where they lived.[3] With the NAACP's leadership, all these families, along with Rev. Brown and his family chose to challenge the system of Jim Crow segregation and consequently give their children an education and life different from theirs growing up.

Public Education in U.S. prior to *Brown I*

The area of public education has had a peculiar past in this country, particularly as it relates to race relations and African Americans. Obviously, during American chattel slavery, enslaved persons were prohibited in many cases by law, from learning to read or write. As discussed in previous chapters, there were those who defied the odds and learned these valuable skills anyway, to author books and essays, as well as the start HBCUSs.

Primary and secondary public education are an entirely different matter. Interestingly, following the Civil War, the Reconstruction Congress required that the former Confederate states in the South provide public education to African Americans, as a condition of readmission to the Union. As a result, states such as South Carolina and Louisiana included provisions prohibiting segregation in their state constitutions. However, these provisions were largely ignored following Reconstruction as these states began to systematically increase the level of segregation between African Americans and whites within their borders.

Toward the end of the 19th century, only Massachusetts outlawed segregation in public schools.[4] After the Civil War, Rhode Island, Michigan, and Connecticut integrated schools, and by the 1870s and 1880s, most of the states in the North prohibited school segregation.[5] In the South, New Orleans was the only place at this time that integrated about 20% of its schools.[6] This lasted only about six years, before the schools were once again re-segregated. As a result of this fact, there was a tremendous increase in African American migration to the North. Ultimately segregation began to rise again in public schools. The decision in *Plessy* only further supported segregation in public schools, although the decision had nothing to do with public education. The combination of *Plessy's* decision permitting segregation in rail cars, with the Court's striking down of the Civil Rights Act of 1875, which prohibited discrimination in public accommodations, only bolstered the states determined to segregate public schools. Thus, as the Supreme Court and the other branches of the federal government were undoubtedly aware, if left to their own devices, the states would ensure that schools and other areas of public life would remain segregated for the foreseeable future. Furthermore, it is interesting that one of the locations for the *Brown I* case was Kansas. This is because of the state's unique historical significance related to slavery. For instance, to replace the Missouri Compromise of 1850, the U.S. Congress passed the Kansas-Nebraska Act. The Missouri Compromise of 1850 was enacted to regulate the number of slave states and free states as Missouri was admitted to the Union. However, it was ultimately ruled unconstitutional by the U.S. Supreme Court in *Dred Scott v. Sandford.*

The Brown Family- Profile in Courage

Rev. Brown was born on August 2, 1918. Rev. Brown and his family's location in the North and in Kansas specifically, is an interesting juxtaposition with the history of African Americans in the South. That also provides interesting context to the *Brown I* case as well, and also one of the reasons that the Topeka case was selected as the lead case. In addition, Rev. Brown's name was strategically selected as the lead name for the Plaintiffs in Topeka. Rev. Brown was born during the period of the Great Migration. This is the period when millions of African Americans escaped the South to the North attempting to find, not necessarily ideal conditions. But better conditions than they and their ancestors had experienced in the South, in the shadow of slavery and the Civil War. Moreover, although Jim Crow made its way up North as well, it is likely that there were greater opportunities, besides farming and an agrarian living, given the advent of the railroad and other industries which began to flourish in the early 1900s. These opportunities also fueled the migration from the South, with the promise of better jobs for African Americans, which could allow them better opportunities to raise their families.

Rev. Brown and his wife Leola Montgomery had three daughters, Linda, the oldest, Terry, and Cheryl. Thus, he had a medium-sized family during that day. Leola stayed home while Rev Brown went to work and, in the process, no doubt they built a strong family. This period was an important time in the life of African Americans in the U.S. After the great migration, and with some successes in terms of higher education, African Americans began to be more affluent, and have not only greater economic power, but also greater political power mostly in the North.

Meanwhile, African Americans were still heavily disenfranchised in the South. In keeping with this phenomenon, African Americans began to demand a quality education for their children so they too could achieve even greater heights than their parents. Rev. Oliver Brown's parents' generation endured the *Plessy* era, and the rise of Jim Crow. At the turn of the 20th century, African Americans saw the erosion of any semblance of equal or civil rights that their parents enjoyed following the Civil War, and during Reconstruction. No greater sign of this existed than the rise of lynchings and the passage of laws in state after state segregating the races, and attempting to preserve the separate-but-equal principle established in *Plessy*. Segregation was firmly the law of the land, but African Americans were beginning to prosper despite segregation. The Supreme Court's mandate of separate but equal in *Plessy*, did not ensure that the school Rev. Brown attended was equal to the school that his white counterparts attended.

Rev. Brown- Boxcar Welder

Rev. Brown was employed as a boxcar welder for the Atchison, Topeka, and Santa Fe railroad company in the 1950's prior to the *Brown I* case. It is not clear when he obtained this position or how he was trained to perform it. However, it garnered him a relatively decent living situated in an integrated community. It appears that Rev. Brown and his family were not relegated to the virtual slums that began to develop in many parts of the country, largely as a result of housing discrimination and other means to further segregate African Americans and whites. In addition, some gains in the labor market were achieved as a result of activists such as A. Philip

Randolph, organizing the Brotherhood of Sleeping Car Porters and receiving union protection, under federal law.

In addition, the railroad had become a burgeoning business by this time, with the rise of the industrial age, creating greater opportunity for more people. This allowed African Americans and others to find jobs more easily, without higher levels of education or training. Rev. Brown took advantage of the opportunities that lay before him in working this job. However, he was still subject to racism and thanks to *Plessy* he would continue to witness segregation when observing the train. The rail cars had been the subject of segregation for almost a half century. Thus, while some things changed, for Rev. Brown, some things stayed the same. As he made the trek to work every day, he had to question whether his children would have different opportunities than him. It is very likely that he, like many African American parents and grandparents prior to and during the modern Civil Rights Movement, wondered whether their children would always have to live under separate-but-equal.

Whether despite their efforts, education, knowledge, and skill, they would still receive lower wages, harsher working conditions, and fewer opportunities for advancement simply due to the color of their skin. Whether they would continue to be relegated to a second-class existence to whites, under the false narrative of equality, which could never be achieved, while the races remained separated. One wonders whether Rev. Brown must have thought about what it would be like one day, if his children would no longer have to suffer under the scar of racism, and segregation, but would be included rather than excluded. Whether history would continue to be written with African Americans as a lesser race, in America. It is worth asking the question whether Rev. Brown had the same reaction later popularized by the great African American writer,

James Baldwin, that to be a relatively conscious Negro in America is to be in a constant state of rage.

But as Baldwin recognized, and Rev. Brown was aware, in many cases, African Americans, under the threat of retribution or violence, would have to suffer in silence. Expression of disdain for segregation and conditions at work, could risk job loss and income for one's family. In fact, for many African American men, at that time and in many cases still, the only places where they could truly express themselves outside of the home, was at the church. Thus, the Black Church, is and has always been the haven for African Americans' expressions of their collective frustration and angst at the conditions of society, and the oppression that they face. It has been a place of inspiration, of courage, of indeed education, and a place to strategize and organize.

Rev. Brown and his wife Leola discussed getting involved in the case and the conclusion was essentially what is the worst that could happen if they joined the other families and challenged segregation in elementary schools? Moreover, African American love has always been a different kind of love. A love in the heart of oppression. The complexities of the African American male going to work in segregated spaces and segregated accommodations, and then coming home to be there for his family, has always been a complex dynamic. The African American male navigates the marginalization of society and avoids showing his true self at work, in public, and anywhere but at home. Then he must remove the mask and get along with his spouse and his family. This dichotomy was not uncommon during Rev. Brown's time. This also further illustrates the Duboisian concept of "double-consciousness" that African Americans experience, being two souls in one dark body. Having to be both African and American at the same time.

Rev. Brown, Assistant Pastor

During the early 20th Century and especially during the modern civil rights movement, the pulpit served not only as a place of power and ecumenical fervor with spiritual emphasis. But it was also a place of leadership and movement gathering. Many of the early civil rights leaders, from Vernon Johns, Ralph Abernathy, Jesse Jackson, and of course the Reverend Dr. Martin Luther King, Jr., were preachers and pastors. There are many reasons for this phenomenon. Not the least of which is the commitment to justice, mercy, and compassion provided by the faith and biblical principles which served as their foundation. Another reason is that throughout African American history, immediately after slavery, ministers were more educated or in some cases the only educated persons in the community. One reason behind this was of course, the existence of prohibitions against African Americans reading or writing or otherwise being educated, in many cases by law. In addition, in many cases, ministers received education in religious texts, which themselves are composed of poetry, history, language, and other areas. Moreover, many African American minister-leaders were educated at HBCUs and PWIs. For instance, Dr. King, learned various theories and philosophies that would inform his activism and eventually become incorporated and implemented into strategies in the Civil Rights Movement.

Also, as ministers, these leaders stood with the moral authority in the community to teach and preach what is right and wrong. Thus, they became prime candidates within which to grow and groom their congregations and by extension their communities to move forward fighting for equality and civil rights in this country. Rev. Brown grew out of that tradition as well. As an ordained minister and assistant pastor in the A.M.E. church he attended with his family, he served in this moral position in the church, in the community, and his home.

In addition, preachers and pastors were connected to some of the other cases that were consolidated with the Topeka case by the U.S. Supreme Court. The niece of the Rev. Dr. Vernon Johns, the pastor of the Dexter Avenue Baptist Church in Montgomery Alabama, prior to Dr. King's pastorate, was instrumental in holding a strike in Washington, D.C., which eventually became part of the case from the District of Columbia. The South Carolina case was also brought with the help of Rev. Joseph A. DeLaine. And eventually, Rev. Brown was recruited to join the twelve other families in Topeka under the leadership of the NAACP to fight against segregation in elementary education.

It is no surprise that ministers could not stand on the dais or in the pulpit every Sunday, knowing that Monday through Saturday, their families had to confront injustice in the form of segregation. How could they in good conscious stand and affirm principles of truth and righteousness, when even in their neighborhoods such unrighteousness continued to flourish without challenge.

Rev. Brown was not alone, other African American children throughout the country went to segregated schools as well. Despite the well-meaning and dedicated teachers in segregated black schools, and no matter how genuine their desire to teach the students, these teachers' ability to teach was limited by the lack of equal funding from the state and adequate books and resources in some cases. All these things helped motivate African American parents including Rev. Brown to make the courageous decision to attempt to enroll their children in the all-white elementary school in Topeka. It is with this same faith that he and other parents in Topeka Kansas, Clarendon County, South Carolina, Washington, D.C., Virginia, and Delaware, decided to work with Thurgood Marshall and the other lawyers at the NAACP Legal Defense Fund to challenge school segregation head-on.

The Miseducation of Rev. Brown

During Rev. Oliver Brown generation, segregated schools was a reality. A couple of generations removed from Rev. Brown's, African Americans had been enslaved. Neither slavery nor segregation are conditions that would any parent would want for their children. Akin to the argument that would eventually be made in the case, attending segregated schools continues the same badge of inferiority which had followed Rev. Brown's generation and previous generations since Africans were brought to this country in chains. While the literal chains had been removed, and it was no longer illegal for African Americans to read, or attend school, they were still not able to enjoy the full benefits of citizenship akin to that of whites during Rev. Brown's life up to the point of the *Brown I* case. Instead, African Americans had to continue to live with the limitations that society, and the law placed on them during this time.

The NAACP had been engaged in a multiyear crusade against segregation prior to the *Brown I* case. Eventually lawyers in Topeka and the NAACP began working with parents of students there and at some point, Rev. Brown became aware of the work of the NAACP, and its lawyers. In addition, more and more African Americans were graduating from HBCUs, and other institutions of higher education. This is due in large part to the work of the NAACP. Moreover, there was an increase in African Americans becoming doctors, lawyers, having more professional positions, and achieving a certain level of prominence in their communities and larger society. It is likely that Rev. Brown dreamed of his daughters becoming great thinkers, and leaders in their community, but he knew it would be difficult to do so, without a solid educational foundation. Thus, desegregating public schools was about more than just their education, it was about them being able to ascend to the highest levels of their professional lives and by extension lifting their communities to even higher heights.

Topeka Kansas- Battleground for Desegregation

Topeka Kansas as a region was an interesting place for Rev. Brown and his family to live. There was still a fair amount of discrimination and violence faced by African Americans in the North and Midwest. Nevertheless, Kansas was not necessarily as committed to segregation as many states in the South. In fact, Kansas was not even as committed to preserving segregation, as the other states that were consolidated in *Brown I* case were. Furthermore, the percentage of the population in Kansas that was African American, was significantly lower than the proportion of the population in South Carolina (70%) and the District of Columbia (45%).[7] In many cases, the Kansas public school system and state government officials in Kansas were not necessarily staunch believers in segregation, but they did perform their duty to defend the *Brown* case, based on Supreme Court precedent. This does not mean that Kansas would have integrated public schools without being required to do so by the U.S. Supreme Court. Chances are that they would not.

The fact that the thirteen families including Rev. Brown had to bring this case in the first place is indicative of the level of reception to the idea of integration as a matter of policy and practice in Kansas. Based on the arguments made in the case, however, it is not clear if many Kansans would have opposed school integration. As previously discussed, not being in favor of integration does not render a state a proponent of segregated schools, and vice versa. Rev. Brown and his family lived in a diverse neighborhood during the time of the *Brown I* case. The mere fact that their neighborhood was diverse distanced Rev. Brown and his family from many African Americans in the South and the North. Even in the North, some

African Americans were relegated to housing projects, referred to as "slums" and "ghettos." In many cases, there was a significant difference between the neighborhoods where African Americans and whites were located.

Moreover, Rev. Brown's daughter Linda played with other white children in the neighborhood, which is also a significant development for the case as well. This fact helps to support the arguments later made by the NAACP during the *Brown I* case, that the ability of children of different races to play together in the streets, is proof that attending the same elementary schools, would not cause mass pandemonium. This also helped to defeat any argument of harm to white children by having to attend school with African American children. Furthermore, this phenomenon underscored the flaws in any legal reasoning for the proposition for keeping white and black children separate in public schools.

Kansas' relationship with the railroad and industry in the 1950's indicates it may have been more progressive economically that many southern states, whose economy relied heavily on the cotton industry prior to the Civil War. This connection to the rail industry also may have had an impact on the opinion of segregation in Kansas, as historically, some railroad companies had been against segregation of railcars due to the increased cost to the railroads of having to provide additional cars for African Americans and whites. Additionally, by the time the *Brown I* case came along, the sentiment began to grow that there was very little justification morally for maintaining segregated public schools.

Kansas was likely closer to this school of thought, than say, South Carolina. With the insistence of NAACP lawyers, for the twelve other families in Topeka and Rev. Brown, however, sentiment alone was not enough. They would no longer wait for the hearts of Kansans to turn around on their own. They realized what Dr. King would eventually observe, that for African Americans seeking equality, "'wait' has almost always meant 'never' and that "justice too long delayed is justice denied."[8] They knew that there would have to be a push, to get the state to do the right thing. In fact, the NAACP and its lawyers for their part required any parents who wished to challenge public school segregation to do so with a direct legal assault on segregation itself, rather than another other strategy. Ultimately, Rev. Brown and the other parents agreed to make that challenge, despite whatever repercussions might ensue.

Public Education in 1950's-Fertile Ground for Change

Public education in the 1950's was much like other areas of society for African Americans. The realm of higher education was dominated by many institutions of higher learning, colleges and universities, graduate and professional schools which educated whites. There were relatively few graduate and professional schools that accepted African Americans. However, numerous historically black colleges and universities educated African American undergraduate students. Although these institutions did not have comparable resources to that of majority institutions, they produced illustrious graduates who would go onto serve their communities. There were some occasions where graduates of HBCUs would go on to apply to graduate and professional programs at majority institutions, only to be denied access based on race. Sadly, *Plessy* was still precedent, and these students were rejected despite being overqualified in some cases and deserving of being admitted based on their own merit. In fact, when the NAACP began challenging segregated admissions practices at graduate and professional schools, they would obtain proof in the form of a letter from the school, verifying that the African American applicants were qualified to attend the schools and would be admitted, but for their race.

Meanwhile, public schools around the country were even more segregated than the institutions of higher education. Based on the Court's decisions pre-*Brown I*, it appeared that the Justices were more comfortable with the integration in higher education than in primary and secondary schools. In addition, when challenged in court, states argued that separate higher education programs and facilities were equal and therefore could remain separate under *Plessy*, to meet the requirements of equal protection under the 14th Amendment. The problem with this argument and the challenge for these states is that their separate facilities were anything but equal.

Prior to *Brown I*, in the South, there were 15 medical schools, 4 dental schools, and 16 law schools that admitted white students. Meanwhile, none of these graduate and professional schools in the South, admitted African Americans.[9] This is crucial, because in 1950, there was no Title VI, or Title IX, or really any law which prohibited discrimination in higher education. The irony is that although *Plessy* involved railroads not education, it was the basis for many states' refusal to desegregate. It was perhaps fortuitous that public education became instrumental in sparking social and racial change, as it would be another 10 and 11 years respectively before passage of the 1964 Civil Rights Act, and the 1965 Voting Rights Act.

Education was also an important battleground, particularly at this time, given the backdrop of World War II, which had been going on in the recent years prior to the 1950s. The war placed a great strain on American welfare and particularly on the U.S. military, which had been integrated almost seven years earlier. Although the U.S. military was fraught with problems of racism even after integration, it was proof that young people of different races could coexist. No matter the segment of society, the arguments against integration had the same theme: African Americans were inferior, by their race, and therefore they should remain separate from whites.

The challenge in maintaining this argument and consequently the reason why it ultimately failed, was that there was no way to divorce the purported African American inferiority from slavery. In fact, this alleged inferiority of people of African ancestry is one of the main justifications given for slavery. Thus, if the descendants of enslaved persons were indeed too inferior to attend schools with whites then the law treated them no better than their enslaved African ancestors. This conclusion would be difficult to sustain given the occurrence of the Civil War and passage of the Civil War Amendments, which were designed to abolish slavery. Taking this argument to its logical conclusion, meant slavery never ended, and Jim Crow segregation was merely another form of slavery. Moreover, although the Court managed to do so for several decades, reconciling the equal protection mandate in the 14th Amendment of the U.S. Constitution, with segregation, eventually proved problematic. Therefore, like most things, the state of public education in the 1950s was complex.

On the other hand, segregation is only part of the story, the inspirational stories of HBCUs was another part. These bastions of African American intellectual thought were also bursting with black culture and history. Most of these institutions had highly qualified faculty, as they could not gain employment at majority institutions, due to employment discrimination. In addition, HBCUs (many of whom were either state supported or supported by a religious institution or organization) filled these roles. They provided both pretextual cover to states fighting against integration in college admissions, and at the same time, provided a place where the black intelligentsia were able to develop and train the next generation of thought leaders and pioneers in African American life.

For instance, the great historian W.E.B. DuBois was educated at an HBCU, Fisk University, before going on to receive his Ph. D, from

Harvard University. Thurgood Marshall carried the baton across the finish line in the legal campaign to end segregation in public education. He went on to serve as a federal judge, U.S. Solicitor General, and an Associate Justice of the U.S. Supreme Court. He was also educated at Lincoln University in Pennsylvania, and Howard University Law School, both HBCUs. In fact, it was at Howard Law School, an HBCU, that Marshall, while a young law student met, learned from, and was mentored by Charles Hamilton Houston, the law school's dean and the architect of the legal strategy to end segregation in higher education and public education.

As an aside, one of the great debates of the time among African Americans, was between Booker T. Washington's Atlanta Compromise doctrine and DuBois' desegregation theory. Both these great leaders and thinkers opposed segregation as a matter of principle, were educators at HBCUs, and were concerned about the future of the race and the country for that matter. Where they differed was likely how African Americans could and would achieve progress in the face of segregation and white supremacy. The legacies of DuBois and Washington were also bright spots in the state of public education before *Brown I*.

The field of education would undergo dramatic changes in terms of legal restrictions before the end of the decade. These changes would have lasting effects on society and send ripples throughout the country and indeed the world. These changes would not be fully implemented for several years, but at least they would begin. The tide in the sea of change had already begun to turn. Moreover, these victories, as all victories do, would lead to greater victories and even greater struggles. But they would give African Americans and those who fought on the side of equal rights the ammunition to help overturn legal obstacles and attempt to bring justice down like a mighty stream.

―― CHAPTER 8 ――

REACHING THE MOUNTAIN TOP

On the Cusp of the Morn'

There have been few times in the life of the U.S. Supreme Court that have elevated the Court beyond its current stature to become something greater. Where the Court transcended law, government, and even the individual Justices. When the Court spoke with one voice for righteousness... for justice... for peace. When it truly embodied the words written over its building, "Equal justice under Law," in the hearts and minds of everyday Americans and even the world. Arguably one of those such moments is, May 17, 1954, beginning almost just before 1:00 pm eastern time, as Chief Justice Earl Warren began reading the decision in what would become to be known as *Brown v. the Board of Education,* or more accurately *Brown I.* The official name of the case, is *Oliver Brown, et al., v. the Board of Education of Topeka Kansas, et al.* The "case" as it is commonly referred to, was actually a total of five cases, which were consolidated together since they raised the same central question, as is common practice. This question which will be discussed later, was famously announced by Chief Justice Warren prior to issuing the

Court's opinion in the case. In addition to the Topeka, Kansas case, the other cases were from the states of Virginia, Delaware, South Carolina, and the District of Columbia.

The Topeka case was chosen because it was first on the docket, and also the Justices wanted to make clear that segregated schools was not just a southern issue. In doing so, the Justices made Rev. Brown and his oldest daughter Linda famous, not only across the country, but throughout history. Their names are forever etched in the history and pantheon of Civil Rights Cases as well as African American history. Although the decision was almost a century in the making, *Brown I*, became the decision where everything changed, but with *Brown II*, everything stayed the same for a while. *Brown I* was a seminal moment and despite its legal authority, it was a moral statement for the Court and the nation.

Indeed, although some may doubt its legal legitimacy, very few if any, doubt *Brown I*'s validity and result. *Brown I* corrects a wrong done long ago. In fact, for those who are critical of the case, *Brown I* would not have been necessary, if not for the other two cases discussed in this book. If there were no *Dred Scott v. Sandford*, nor *Plessy v. Ferguson*, then *Brown I* would not have been needed. No, this case was bigger than public education, bigger than just the five cases that made it up. *Brown I* was the result of a 25-year campaign, or rather battle waged in the courts, by the NAACP and its legal team.

For all the praise and attention, it rightfully received, the strategy behind *Brown I*, was very nuanced and the result of a larger and more sophisticated overall legal strategy, beginning with *Sweatt v. Painter*. *Sweatt* involved a legal challenge to the University of Texas Law School's denial of Mr. Heman Sweatt from admission, based on his race, under *Plessy v. Ferguson*. For the first time, the U.S. Supreme Court ordered that Sweatt must be admitted to the University of Texas Law School, as relief in the case.[1] This was a major departure from previous cases where the U.S. Supreme Court had simply ordered the state to make efforts to either create a new separate institution for African Americans, or update the inferior facilities that had been created to avoid integrating the white institution, as in the case of *Sipuel v. the University of Oklahoma*.[2] In addition, there were some cases, such as in *Murray vs. Pearson*, where Maryland state courts ruled that state educational institutions could not deny admission to applicants based on race under the Fourteenth Amendment, and eventually the state would give up the fight and integrate the University of Maryland Law School.[3]

Sweatt, was the first time, that the Court appeared prepared to affirmatively order desegregation in the field of public higher education. All these cases followed the strategy of arguing that the separate schools were not equal in facilities, resources, faculty, etc., and therefore the states had to either make them equal or admit the African American applicants. The genius behind this strategy was to point out that these makeshift institutions were merely a pretext to try to comply with *Plessy*'s mandate, and avoid desegregation. Not only that, but this strategy also opened the minds of segregationist state government leaders who realized that "manufacturing" law schools, medical schools, and other institutions of higher education required enormous resources and capital. They had to come to terms with the requirement of spending significant resources just to avoid allowing the admission of one or a few African American students.

At this point, the strategy was not to attack *Plessy* directly, although that may have been the goal. Instead, it was to show that *Plessy* was an unworkable solution practically, and unsound principle legally. Moreover, the strategy was a methodical approach which turned on the facts of each case. This allowed the Courts to feel more comfortable in ruling in favor of these individual applicants. Thus, the ruling by the U.S. Supreme Court that the state of Texas must admit Sweatt into its law school, was quite different from declaring segregation to be unconstitutional. Therefore, the NAACP began building momentum toward *Brown I*, long before the case itself. Along the way, Charles Hamilton Houston and Thurgood Marshall collected information, brought in documentation, and obtained expert testimony, to help sway the Court in many of these cases.

What makes the legal strategy of the NAACP lawyers even more brilliant, was that although desegregation in public education, in *Brown I* was their ultimate target, they managed to knock down many other targets along the way. They realized that *Brown I*, was a multi-year, even multi-decade fight, and that it was a journey rather than a destination. As will be discussed later, despite the fact that *Brown I* may have been providential, the case was not necessarily mystical in its development.

Legal Background of the Case
The Whole is Equal to the Sum of its Parts

One of the more difficult cases, in the five cases that made up *Brown I*, is the case from Clarendon County, South Carolina. In that case, Reverend Joseph A. DeLaine, Levi Pearson, and Harry Briggs, Sr, were involved in Harry Briggs' son being allowed to integrate an elementary school.[4] Thurgood Marshall and the NAACP legal team, argued the pretrial hearing in the South Carolina case, on November 17, 1950, before U.S. District Judge Waties Waring.[5] Marshall and these plaintiffs knew that theirs was a difficult task, particularly in South Carolina, a place where segregation and racism was prevalent. The case was *Briggs* (for Harry Briggs, Sr., on behalf of his son, Harry Briggs, Jr.) *v. R. W. Elliott*, (the chairman of the Board of Trustees of School District No. 22). The lawsuit claimed that the board failed to provide sufficient school facilities for the African

American students of Clarendon County, South Carolina. Besides the Topeka and Clarendon County cases, there were *Davis v. County School Board of Prince Edward County* (Virginia),[6] *Gebhart v. Belton* (Delaware),[7] and *Bolling v. Sharpe* (District of Columbia) (as mentioned earlier this case was brought by the niece of Rev. Vernon Johns, predecessor to Dr. Martin Luther King, Jr. as pastor of the historic Dexter Avenue Baptist Church in Montgomery, Alabama).[8]

Plessy Yesterday, Plessy Today

Under the Judiciary Act of 1937, constitutional challenges to state law in federal court, were required to be heard by a three-judge panel of U.S. District Judges.[9] The case of *Briggs v. Elliott* challenged segregation in public education under the Fourteenth Amendment of the U.S. Constitution and thus, was heard by a three-judge panel. In addition to Judge Waring, the other two members of the three-judge panel were Judges George Bell Timmerman (another U.S. District Court Judge in South Carolina), and John J. Parker, (who at the time was the chief judge of the U.S. Court of Appeals for the Fourth Circuit).[10] Regardless of who the judges were, on this challenge to segregated public schools in South Carolina, there was one major problem precedentially and practically. Namely the case which stood as the highest obstacle for the *Brown I* case: *Plessy v. Ferguson*. Even though this case had nothing to do with public education, or anything else outside of railcar segregation, this case was the valley that the lawyers and families in *Brown I* would have to travel through in order to reach the mountaintop for victory. For *Brown I* to live, *Plessy* had to die. This was the only way; they could not coexist.

Despite the *Plessy* obstacle, there were still some good caselaw on the side of the Plaintiffs in South Carolina and other places. Cases like *Sweatt*, and *Sipuel* were instrumental in at least making the

Justices and the states rethink segregation, although not enough to overturn *Plessy*. In addition, in South Carolina, there was enormous support for segregation, as like many in the South, and some in the North, relying on *Plessy*, the state passed segregationist laws excluding African Americans from various sectors of society. For these reasons, the NAACP legal team, and Thurgood Marshall were not optimistic about a victory in South Carolina, but hoped to use it as ammunition in the eventual case to be brought before the U.S. Supreme Court. In fact, while the Court was still considering the South Carolina case, Thurgood Marshall and the NAACP legal team were preparing to go to Topeka to try the case involving Rev. Oliver and Linda Brown, as they believed that Kansas might be a great case for the overall legal strategy.[11]

Speaking of the Commonwealth of Virginia, this was birthplace of American chattel slavery (in Jamestown in 1619), the cradle of slavery, the capital of the Confederacy, (in Richmond, in 1861), and the site of the final surrender of the Civil War, by the South (in Appomattox County, Virginia, in 1865). Indeed, home to General Lee himself, Virginia has always had a precarious position with respect to African Americans and segregation. It is for this reason, that the Virginia case has special meaning as one of the cases challenging segregation in public education. Furthermore, Virginia would join another southern state, South Carolina to challenge segregation, despite the stronghold of Jim Crow laws in the South. The District of Columbia case was a little different, in that it was the only case initially brought by the parents of the students themselves, rather than the NAACP. This fact alone distinguishes the District of Columbia case from the other cases. In addition, the District of Columbia was not a state, (a point about which many of its residence decry) and thus, likely had a different trajectory in technical terms from cases from the other actual states. The last case, in Delaware, like the Kansas case, was from a northern state and helped to contrast *Brown I* as more than just a southern challenge to segregation. These northern cases, in the NAACP and the Court's eyes, helped to demonstrate the national importance of the case for desegregation in public education.

Case History

Just like the *Briggs* case in Clarendon County, South Carolina, the Topeka Kansas case, and indeed in all the other cases, except Delaware, there was a three-judge panel which reviewed each of the cases in their respective federal districts. The cases were appealed to the Courts of Appeals, and not surprisingly in each case, the federal district and appeals courts ruled against the Plaintiffs and in favor of the states involved and the District of Columbia. Of note, in the Delaware case, the Court of Chancery ruled in favor of the Plaintiffs, but of course, the defendants appealed the case, and it was ultimately heard along with the other four cases by the U.S. Supreme Court. Similarly, in Topeka Kansas, despite acknowledging *Plessy* as controlling, the three-judge panel placed in the record and recognized the negative effects of segregation on African American children. These developments were an important fact and one which forebode the ultimate result of the case, despite the long journey. Moreover, they represented the different views of some states, like Kansas and Delaware toward segregation in public education. As the NAACP had predicted, states like these might be more vulnerable to challenging segregation in public schools.

First Argument

Lawyers for the States

Upon reaching the U.S. Supreme Court, as had been widely anticipated, the lead counsel for the states, in addition to their respective attorneys general was John W. Davis, an experienced litigator with an impressive record of success arguing before the U.S. Supreme Court. He was brought in not only for his legal skill, but also because of his background in the South, and his ability to intelligently and legitimately argue on behalf of segregation, regardless of his personal feelings on the subject. Moreover, he was well-respected by the Court and many in the legal profession, and this was also deemed a reason to select Mr. Davis, as an effective advocate in *Brown I*. With his historic record and legal ability, Mr. Davis had been solicitor general and even could have been a member of the Court. Thus, the states, chose well in their selection of Mr. Davis to argue such an important case.

Lawyers for the Plaintiffs

While the attorney for the States or Respondents, was widely experienced as an advocate before the U.S. Supreme Court, the lead attorney for the Plaintiffs, Thurgood Marshall was becoming a legal and appellate rising star in his own right, beginning to amass a respectable win-loss record before the U.S. Supreme Court. His victories were beginning to pile up, and even John Davis took notice of Thurgood's potential and ability. Thurgood's inspiration for *Brown I*, began in his own educational life. As a native of Baltimore, he naturally wanted to attend the University of Maryland Law School, which like Linda Brown, was near his home. However, also like Linda Brown's neighborhood school, the University of Maryland did not admit African Americans to its law school. Thus, Thurgood, like young, Linda, would have to travel (in Thurgood's case over an hour one-way) to attend the struggling Howard Law School.

But something amazing happened. Almost providentially, a divine connection was created when the young Mr. Marshall met the distinguished Dean Charles Hamilton Houston. Dean Houston became a teacher and trusted mentor to Thurgood, and Thurgood became his star pupil at Howard Law School. This bond would continue after law school when Houston convinced Marshall to join him in his work at the NAACP. Together they forged through segregated town after segregated town gathering plaintiffs and amassing evidence to support their legal challenges. In fact, after Dean Houston could no longer lead the NAACP legal team, Marshall would take over for his former mentor, professor, and law school dean.

Government's Position

The solicitor general at the time of *Brown I* who argued before the Supreme Court was Simon Sobeloff. The government's brief was supportive of the Plaintiffs in the case. By the time the case got to the Supreme Court, sentiment had changed regarding segregation, and following several of the other cases to consider public education by the Supreme Court, it was clear that society had begun to turn toward integration in other facets of society, and that public education would likely be next.

Second Argument

Question Presented

When it agreed to hear the *Brown I* cases, the U.S. Supreme Court likely knew that there would be great pressure and attention placed on the Court. This contributed to the hesitancy of the members of the Court, and combined with the issues involved, likely resulted in the Court ordering a second oral argument in the next term, and having the parties answer additional questions. The re-argument was centered around the conditions that existed at the time of the adoption of the 14th Amendment. Specifically, the Court asked the parties, and the U.S. Attorney General's office to brief and be prepared to argue six questions one of which asked, "What evidence is there that the Congress which submitted, and the State Legislatures and conventions which ratified the Fourteenth Amendment contemplated or did not contemplate, understood or did not understand, that it would abolish segregation in public schools?"[12]

The other five questions dealt primarily with the relief the Court could or should award, in the (likely) event of a ruling that segregation in public schools was unconstitutional. The fact that all but one of the Court's questions for the parties and others involved, dealt with an appropriate remedy for the Plaintiffs was an indication that the Court was likely to overturn *Plessy*. Moreover, what worried the Justices more than the constitutional question, was how to implement the answer to that question. The state of the country, especially the South, which had been particularly recalcitrant in the area of segregation in public education, was very much top of mind of the Justices of the Court. Moreover, one of the counter-arguments that the States and their representatives made against the Plaintiffs in *Brown I*, was that the Court either had no power to grant the Plaintiffs what they wanted, or they could not fashion an appropriate remedy for the Plaintiffs.

Court's Composition

As has been widely reported, there is a great deal of debate about whether at the time of the first oral argument or the second, there were five solid votes to overturn *Plessy* and declare segregation in public schools violated the Constitution. There were significant doubts about the likelihood that Justices Jackson and Reed, as well as Chief Justice Fred Vincent, would vote for desegregation. Nevertheless, in the time between the second oral argument and the Court's rendering its decision, Chief Justice Fred Vinson passed away unexpectedly. Thus, leaving a vacancy on the Court. President Dwight D. Eisenhower did not delay but appointed a former governor of California, some suspect, to curry favor with the California delegation and help bolster him in the upcoming Presidential election. Thus, Chief Justice Earl Warren was appointed to replace the former Chief Justice. One interesting note about Chief Justice Warren, is that in addition to serving as the former governor of the largest state in the U.S., he also previously served as a District Attorney, also an elected position. As a former politician, Chief Justice Warren was likely experienced in building consensus, and very concerned about the public's opinion of the case. Furthermore, he was very attentive to the moment in which he now found himself, at the very center of one of the most important Supreme Court cases in the Court's history.

This was not lost on Chief Justice Warren, as it appears that he used his political negotiation skills to help convince the other members of the Court, who were still likely on the fence or solidly against overturning *Plessy*. He knew it was important for the Court to speak as one, and that a divided Court, even one who ruled in favor of the Plaintiffs would just deepen the rift in the country on this issue. By that, Chief Justice Warren likely hit the ball out of the park. On the other hand, he displayed further political attributes, by an also unanimous decision in *Brown II*, with the declaration of the desegregation of public schools proceeding, "with all deliberate speed."[13] There are those who surmise that had Chief Justice Vinson lived, he may or may not have ruled in favor of the Plaintiffs. At the very least he likely would not have taken the time and effort to corral the other Justices to a unanimous opinion, overturning *Plessy*. Marshall knew that the former Chief Justice would not have been a supporter of the Plaintiffs' position. Although, some in the legal academy dispute the merits of the claim that Chief Justice Vinson would have voted against overturning *Plessy,* and he had voted in favor of the NAACP in earlier desegregation cases, including *Sweatt* and *Sipuel,* which were discussed earlier. Nevertheless, Chief Justice Warren's selection was a success for the Plaintiffs, as well as for civil rights and civil liberties across the country. It has been reported that President Eisenhower thought the opinion in *Brown I*, was wrongly decided, and in fact was reluctant to enforce the decision once it was issued by the Court.

Changing Public Opinion

There is little doubt in the literature, in the reflections of those who were there, and based on accounts from those who preserved their commentary for future generations, that the public opinion on desegregation of public schools was beginning to change. Also, as discussed earlier, many states were forced to establish separate institutions of higher education and/or graduate and professional schools, whether based on costs or litigation. Either way, African Americans were beginning to attend schools with whites in various areas across the country.

Thus, it was becoming increasingly clear that the Supreme Court's decision in *Brown I*, would not necessarily be a surprise. The question was whether the Court would issue the decision itself and whether there was the judicial and political will to overturn *Plessy*.

In addition, some of that force was brought upon by actual or threatened litigation. In fact, in the 70 years since the end of the Civil War, 44 lawsuits were filed challenging segregated education at all levels.[14] Thus, the issue would no longer be ignored, if it ever was so, in the first place, and as a result, more and more integration seemed to be a likely possibility. Some have argued that the Supreme Court was given too much credit for *Brown I*. The contention is that the Court was too slow in ending segregation in public schools, and only did so, when the Plaintiffs, the NAACP, and the practical realities of society demanded this result. This brings to mind the quote from, Albion Tourgée about the Court. Whether the Court decided *Brown I*, based on moral integrity, judicial activism, or mere coalescence, the result was in the making even if it took years to fully complete. In fact, the number of white southerners who supported integration rose from 1 in 50 in 1942 to 1 in 7 in 1956.[15]

Behind the Scenes of the Case
Providence or Prescience

Some proponents of *Brown I*, have argued that all the stars aligned in order to produce the result that was achieved. They believe that it was a perfect storm. Some, including a member of the Court believed it was the result of divine intervention. Nevertheless, what is clear is that the Court was poised to decide the *Brown I* case, given the previous cases that it had considered. Moreover, the Court specifically reserved the question of revisiting *Plessy*, until later.

In fact, based on records of memos during the time of the first conference, the unofficial tally among the Justices, was Black, Burton, Minton, and Douglas in favor of integration, while Vinson, Reed, and Clark were leaning toward upholding *Plessy*. Meanwhile, Frankfurter and Jackson also thought that segregation was constitutional, but they were hesitant to decide the issue at the time, given the condition of the country.[16] After the passing of Chief Justice Vinson, and the appointment of Chief Justice Warren, the new Chief Justice was very active in attempting to get the Court to decide the case unanimously. Moreover, Chief Justice Warren began to read many sources, including Gunnar Mydal's *An American Dilemma* (1944), which forecasted and ultimately influenced the Chief Justice's decision to vote to end segregation in public education.

A Lawyer's Journey

Thurgood Marshall eventually became the first African American Supreme Court justice in American History. He was also the first

African American Solicitor General. Prior to that he was a federal judge on the 2nd Circuit Court of Appeals. But before all these high-ranking positions, he was the "Negro lawyer." He had been trained by the best, Dean Charles Hamilton Houston, and he cut his teeth defending African Americans falsely accused of crimes and filing lawsuits seeking to end discrimination. As an appellate advocate he won 29 out of the 32 cases he argued before the U.S. Supreme Court. He became the most famous African American lawyer or lawyer of any race for that matter, in history. His journey took him from a Baltimore middle class neighborhood all the way to the highest court in the land. Everything that he learned, every danger that he faced, all the trips that he took with Dean Houston throughout the south and across the country, gathering plaintiffs and evidence, built up to this moment. The time was now.

~Lead Counsel in Brown v. Board of Education case, Associate U.S. Supreme Court Justice Thurgood Marshall – Courtesy Library of Congress~

Fears of the Crowd

The Supreme Court was very concerned about the state of the country surrounding race relations, in 1954. They were also concerned about violence, hate, and what would happen across the country if their decision was not well received. They were concerned about the southern reaction, and the resistance to desegregation from states in the South. The Court was afraid of being thrust into the battle between the rights of African Americans, and the status of Jim Crow segregation, that its decision in *Plessy* helped to cement in this country. But there were also members of the Court who were concerned about what would happen if the Court upheld *Plessy*. Would the Supreme Court once again usher in a new century of segregation and division between the races? Up until the time of *Brown I*, the Court had been able to make very limited holdings in cases based on the facts in those cases, without having to speak directly to the issue of segregation, and by extension white supremacy. The more conservative members of the Court were always concerned about being seen as judicial activists and wading into the purview of Congress. They were concerned that the Court might engage in making law, or holding what the law should be, without regard or respect to what the law is.

In fact, when the Court agreed to hear the cases, it was decided that Kansas should be placed at the top of the docket, to ensure that the case would not be considered merely a southern case.[17] Moreover, by the time of *Brown I*, the Equal Protection Clause of the 14th Amendment had been largely ignored for almost 90 years. This allowed segregation to flourish, particularly in the South.[18] In addition, lynchings soared to an all-time high in the 1890's.[19] All of these things were likely on the dashboard of many of the Justices' minds when they agreed to hear *Brown I*, including two oral arguments.

The Decision

The Opinion

At approximately, 12:52 pm, on Monday, May 17, 1954, Chief Justice Earl Warren, began reading what would become one of, if not the most famous decision in the history of the U.S. Supreme Court.[20] The Chief Justice indicated that the five cases, from the states of Kansas, South Carolina, Virginia, Delaware, and the District of Columbia, had been consolidated as they all raised the same question. All but the Delaware case, were reversed, as the Delaware Supreme Court allowed African American students admission to white schools, despite acknowledging that *Plessy* was still the law of the land.[21]

What differentiated these cases from previous cases the Court decided in the area of public education? Previous cases challenged the lack of equality in the facilities between African Americans and whites. The cases that comprised *Brown I*, challenged whether segregation itself was incompatible with the mandate of the 14th Amendment's equal protection clause. Chief Justice Warren went on to give some background of the cases. He also referenced that the results of briefing and arguments regarding the original intent of the 14th Amendment and segregation in public education were inconclusive at best. And of course, he referenced the obstacle of *Plessy* as precedent in the case and the fact that previous cases, including in higher education where the court found segregation unconstitutional, left *Plessy* in place temporarily. In his opinion he also referred to psychological evidence which was presented by the Plaintiffs that supported the contention that segregation harmed African American students merely by the fact that they were segregated.

Furthermore, the Chief Justice went on to discuss the importance of an education in American society in 1954, its necessity, and the resources undertaken by the state to provide an education to its children. The Chief Justice continued that the Court cannot return to 1868, to determine what the 14th Amendment meant when it was passed and ratified, nor could the Court travel back to 1896 to examine *Plessy*. Instead, Chief Justice Warren indicated that public education is a right, and a State's denial of this right to certain students based solely on their race, was unconstitutional. The Court concluded by deciding that the Plaintiffs were only denied entrance into public schools with whites solely because of their race. Then the Chief Justice uttered, his most important statement from the opinion. "We conclude that, in the field of public education, the doctrine of "separate but equal" has no place. Separate educational facilities are inherently unequal."[22]

Speaking as One

The politician in Chief Justice Warren recognized the importance of the decision in *Brown I*. He was keenly aware of what a divided decision even one finding in favor of the Plaintiffs would do. Even with unanimity, there were those who doubted the Court's ruling, believed that the Court would change its mind back, or that the decision would one day be reversed.[23] But the Chief Justice was adamant that the decision be unanimous to send a clear message to the country, and indeed the world, regarding segregation at least in public education. Given the importance of the decision, there has been speculation since the case was decided, about which Justices wanted to rule in favor of segregation. In addition, there have been controversies over future Supreme Court Justices who drafted briefs in support of maintaining segregation, while they were judicial clerks at the time of the *Brown I* decision. People tend not to want to be on the wrong side of history if they can avoid it. Therefore, it is not surprising that there are conflicting reports about which

Justices wanted to dissent from the majority. Nevertheless, the Chief Justice ruled the day and the case goes down in history as a unanimous ruling which echoed throughout the courthouses, legislatures, and schoolhouses of the country.

Legal Precedent or Social Experiment

For all that *Brown I* stood and still stands for today, there are those with lingering questions regarding the case. Some critics of *Brown I*, express doubts, not about the conclusion, but how the Court arrived at its decision. Of note, is the Court's apparent reliance on psychological data presented by the Plaintiffs, as expressed through the Chief Justice's opinion. Particularly, the experiment by Drs. Clark, which examined several African American children using white dolls and black dolls. The Clark experiment illustrated the identity complex that had developed within the African American students toward themselves and white students simply by being segregated at school.[24] The Supreme Court made note of this harm, which coincided with the findings of the three-judge panel in the Topeka, Kansas case, that segregation had an adverse effect on the African American students.[25]

Although the Court had requested briefing by the parties and other participants in the case on the question of the congressional intent behind the 14th Amendment, it did not deal with the legal precedent in any meaningful way. It is not that there was no legal precedent necessarily, nor that the Court did not believe that the decision was based on solid legal grounds. It appears that the Chief Justice and the Court were more concerned about having an opinion that lay people could understand. The Court clearly did not want to issue an opinion that was based in legal jargon. Instead, the Court wanted to issue a decision that the southern legislator or school administrator, as well as the northern stay-at-home parent or businessperson could understand. The Court was keenly aware that its decision would have long-lasting effects and would be read by thousands of people at the time, and by even more people in the future. It appears that the Justices wanted to ensure that all people who read the decision would understand that they were not deciding just a legal question, but a moral question that went to the very heart of American ideals. Apparently, the Court declared with one loud voice that segregation in public education was inconsistent with both the letter and the spirit of the Constitution.

The Most Powerful Line in the World

Seven words, spoken with the stern tone of the Chief Justice of the Supreme Court of the United States. These words sounded like the voice of a lark heralding the morning dew for many African Americans. Words that would inspire a generation as well as spark and energize a movement. The Court could have rendered its decision without uttering these words, but the Chief Justice clearly thought that it was necessary to leave no room for doubt, conjecture, misunderstanding, or misstatement of their ruling. The Court's strong words resonated throughout the country and the South, especially. After announcing this huge declaration, the Court proceeded to deal with the legal ramifications of its decision. The Delaware case, the only one where the Delaware Chancery Court ordered integration, but upheld *Plessy*, was affirmed, but remanded based on the Court's overruling itself on *Plessy*. All four remaining cases were reversed and remanded to the District Courts, for proceedings also to be consistent with the Court's overruling of *Plessy*.

The Court advised that the Plaintiffs, and all those similarly situated were denied the equal protection of the law, although it would have to be enforced in later decisions, which will be discussed further in this book. The Court made clear that even though these cases came from only 4 states and the District of Columbia, its decision would apply nationwide. Therefore, segregation anywhere in public education was now unconstitutional. The Court reached beyond the hesitation of its members and may not have fully grasped the task ahead for the Court and its lower courts to implement its ruling. The Court did not listen to the naysayers who barked that it had no power to issue such a ruling or that it lacked the ability or mechanism to enforce its decision. The Court reached past all these obstacles and arrived at likely its greatest conclusion.

Perhaps the Chief Justice and some of the other Justices remembered some of the earlier decisions, like *Plessy* and others, which set the country back decades in their own way. With *Brown I*, they were trying to move the country forward. It is possible that the Court was aware of the damage done first by *Dred Scott* and then *Plessy*, even though some argue that segregation could have flourished without *Plessy*. Perhaps the Court thought that *Plessy* tipped the scales so to speak in favor of segregation, and that *Brown I*, tipped the scales back in balance. In any event the Court stood up for the African American child Plaintiffs, and the entire African American race. The Court was aware of the horrors that segregation and white supremacy had borne on African American citizens. They were also aware of the reluctance of some in the white population and the staunch segregationists who would rail against the decision. In this moment the Court interpreted the Constitution based on the ideals that the 14th Amendment represented when it was adopted. Even though it may not have said so explicitly, the Court also interpreted the Constitution with the ideals that it believed the country stood for in 1954. The Court was clear and emphatic that segregation in public education no longer has a place in American society. The interesting thing is that the Court did so, without denigrating its prior brethren who issued *Plessy*, it merely spoke with one voice that *Plessy* was no more.

CHAPTER 9

THE STRUGGLE CONTINUES

Brown, A Many Splendored Thing
Criticisms of the Brown I Decision

For all that *Brown I* was, almost as quickly as it became a hallmark moment, it was the subject of criticism from many politicians, government officials, and school administrators. The case was criticized in part based on the data upon which the Court relied. Throughout history legal scholars have debated the propriety of the Court's mention of the psychological experiment on African American children. The Court referenced the evidence, in what has become the infamous footnote 11 to the opinion. This footnote has been highly criticized by detractors of the *Brown I* case in some respects for the fact that many doubted the basis and findings of the psychological experiment.

In addition, another principal criticism focused on the Court's reliance on sociological evidence, rather than legal precedent or case law. In this way, the Court's decision in *Brown I* was regarded by some as judicial activism and a departure from previous rulings of the Court.[1] The interesting thing about this particular criticism is that it fails to consider the fact that the Court has historically considered similar evidence at different points in time in different cases, as support for its decisions. Furthermore, the Court had engaged in a similar process, in the *Lochner v. New York* case, and many of its anti-New Deal cases.[2] Moreover, there is nothing to suggest that the Court was prohibited from relying on such evidence it considered relevant.

Perhaps part of the reason that those who criticized the *Brown I* decision, did so was because they wanted the Court's decision to be immune from questions about the validity of the decision, especially in the South. An interesting counterargument to these criticisms of the *Brown I* decision is that *Plessy*, the case *Brown I*, ultimately overturned, was likely unsupported by legal precedent. In addition, many of the laws that were enacted after *Plessy* using it as a basis, were consequently also unsupported by the law. Hence, if *Plessy* was indeed wrongly decided, which not many people now doubt, then all the segregationist laws that were passed in response to *Plessy* were also legally unsound.[3] Thus, *Brown I* was necessary to correct the Court's mistake in *Plessy*. Moreover, *Dred Scott*, which was the first case discussed in this book, was also not only unsupported by precedent, but it was largely an extraneous opinion given that the Court determined that the Scotts were not citizens and that federal courts likely lacked jurisdiction to hear and decide the case.

Rising Doubts

In addition to criticisms regarding the merits of the case itself, there also those in 1954, who had serious doubts about the practicality of the decision. For staunch segregationists and white supremacists, open and adamant objection to the decision rang out. Not only did many in the South object to the decision, but many were also against desegregation at all. There was no shortage of people willing to provide commentary about the *Brown I* decision. For instance, years after *Brown I*, the Governor of Arkansas, Orville Faubus, remarked that he was not bound by the decision. Thus, he denied several African American children the ability to attend a white school in Little Rock, Arkansas. Thereafter, the Court in a subsequent case ruled that he and others were bound by the *Brown I* decision, and the students were admitted over Governor Faubus' objection. These first children became to be known as the Little Rock Nine.

But Governor Faubus was not alone, U.S. Senator Robert Byrd, of Virginia remarked that he believed the Court would reverse the decision. However, not all officials would voice skepticism at the decision. Governor Fob James, Sr., of Alabama declared that the Supreme Court's decision in *Brown I* was the law and that it must be followed. This of course, did not mean that schools would be willing to integrate without a fight. Instead, the path to integration would be a long and hard-fought battle.

The Chief Justice's idea to write the *Brown I* decision in the way that he did, appears to have been that it was not enough to merely issue an opinion ruling against segregation in public schools. Instead, he hoped that if he injected a human element into the opinion, the small children in the experiment, that could assist in swaying people's sentiment toward the decision. It certainly can be argued that merely citing caselaw and legal precedent would not have had the same effect on everyday Americans. The other side of the coin could follow that it would not be enough to merely declare in principal that segregation was unconstitutional. Crafting the remedy in *Brown I*, would be difficult given the enormity of the problem. As will follow, this remedy became the subject of great debate and criticism as well.

Chief Justice Earl Warren ~ Courtesy Library of Congress

Brown II, Victory from the Jaws of Defeat

When the Court initially agreed to hear the *Brown I* case, it was almost a foregone conclusion that there would have to be at least one additional case. Moreover, the Court's questions to the parties for the re-argument were primarily focused on the remedy, if any, the Court could impose. In the *Brown I* opinion itself, in the last paragraph the Court signaled what was to come, and in the same opinion, took the crux of the victory that the Plaintiffs and the NAACP had just secured, right out from under them. What had been the brightest light in the Court's decisions thus far, had already begun to dim.

The Court reserved the question of an appropriate remedy to implement its decision in *Brown I*, in the form of consent decrees, for instance, and invited the parties, the U.S. Justice Department, and states' attorneys' generals to participate in briefing the appropriate remedy for *Brown I*.[4] Much of the Justices' hesitation was based on fear of the repercussions of the decision throughout the nation. The Justices were afraid that if they ordered immediate desegregation, there could be mass resistance which could plunge the country into an even greater divide and possibly turn terribly violent. Their fear is likened to that which existed surrounding the end of slavery and the beginning of Reconstruction. Whether this fear is warranted is subject to debate. But based on the questions asked for re-argument, as well as the discussions between the Justices which have been made public, there was great apprehension at the time *Brown I* was decided. Of course, this apprehension became embodied in *Brown II*, decided the next year in 1955.[5] The states of Florida, North Carolina, Arkansas, Oklahoma, Maryland, and Texas, all filed briefs and participated in oral arguments in *Brown II*.[6]

More specifically the Court's apprehension about a remedy, was evident in its pronouncement, unanimously, in *Brown II*, that school districts were to desegregate "with all deliberate speed."[7] The case was then remanded to the lower courts that originally heard them, as the Court recognized desegregation attempts in Kansas, Delaware, and the District of Columbia.[8] As a result, the Court essentially left the decision, the timing, and the process of desegregation, to the individual school districts who had previously perpetuated a system of segregation. The only check on this ability would be the federal district court judges in the federal judicial districts where the school districts were located.

Thus, the U.S. Supreme Court made a unanimous triumphant decision for the Plaintiffs in *Brown I*, but in *Brown II*, they relinquished its power to individual U.S. District Court judges to determine how to implement their decision in *Brown I*. The language of "all deliberate speed" gave license to segregationist school boards and administrators to delay and obstruct efforts to desegregate public schools. While the Court's sentiment may have been in the right place, the ultimate practical effect of the *Brown II* decision was to roll back the efforts to desegregate schools. The Court's concern in *Brown I* and *II*, were well founded. The South did not react kindly to the decision. Instead, in many places, opponents began efforts to ensure that *Brown I* wasn't enforced, including resorting to violence if necessary, in hopes of maintaining the segregation status quo.

All...deliberate...speed. These three words, so simple, yet at the same time, so powerful. Indeed, the Court was not required to issue this mandate with such vague language. In fact, the Court could have implemented the *Brown I* decision immediately as the NAACP had proposed. In the alternative, the Court could have set a deadline for implementation, as the U.S. Justice Department proposed.[9] But the Court essentially, chose a third, option, which did neither. In so doing, the Court set the country almost as far back in *Brown II*, as it had pushed it forward in *Brown I*. In the Court's mind this may have seemed to be the path of least resistance, and while that may have been true to preserve the Court's stature in the eyes of Americans, it had the opposite effect. Instead of heeding the Supreme Court's call for speed, many across the country, especially in the South took the Court's language as approval of their delay in any way that they could fashion. Whether this was the Court's intended result, may never be known.

Reactions to the Decision

Brown Family

The *Brown I* decision reverberated throughout the country. It seemed that nearly everyone had an opinion, comment, or reaction to the decision. The most earnest and special reactions to the decision belonged to the Brown family, the Briggs family, and all the other Plaintiffs and their families that took part in the *Brown I* case. In addition, all the African American families whose children would no longer be relegated to unequal schools and facilities, also were very happy about the result in the case. But in the Brown family, Rev. Oliver Brown to be exact, responded in the best way he knew how. He thanked God. After news of the decision broke, Linda later recalled her father, exclaiming, "Thanks be to God for this!"[10] As a believer, an ordained minister, and an associate pastor in his church, Rev. Brown could respond in no other way. For many have remarked that the result in *Brown I*, was indeed divinely inspired. He was excited and jovial that his courageous act was rewarded with at least a partial victory. In Linda Brown's case, she began 7th grade at an integrated junior high school.[11] Her father's dream had become a reality, and now his younger daughters would not have to attend segregated schools either. It was a hard-fought victory, one that was years in the making. With the landmark ruling in *Brown I*, their name, and Linda's name would forever be associated with the case and would go down in history books everywhere. Their story would be told for countless generations to come.

The Press

As can be predicted, unlike in *Plessy*, *Brown I*, was highly covered by the press. The Cincinnati Enquirer remarked that *Brown I*"[was]... an act as to the conscience of the American nation."[12] The Chicago

Defender, a very prominent African American newspaper at that time, remarked that it was "a second emancipation proclamation.. [and] it was more important to our democracy than the atomic bomb or the hydrogen bomb."[13] In addition, all African American newspapers were not as enthusiastic about the *Brown I* decision. The Atlanta Journal Constitution indicated that Georgians should "think clearly," likely inviting a certain degree of skepticism in the African American community, about whether the decision would actually lead to the desegregation of schools, or whether this decision while correct in principle, would ever become reality for their lives.

Southern Reaction

As indicated above, there were many doubters and critics of the *Brown I* case, especially from elected officials, particularly in the South. Governor Almond of Virginia believed that *Brown I* would eventually be reversed.[14] Regarded by many as the Segregation Czar, Willie Rainoob, predicted the same. When asked about the Brown I decision, a white supremacist publication declared that the U.S. Supreme Court has reversed itself in the past, and at other times, it completely ignored previous decisions.[15] In addition, a Gallup Poll, indicated that the number of white southerners believing that desegregation was inevitable fell from 55% in 1956 to 43% in 1957.[16] Although, not all southern elected officials had an antagonistic reaction to *Brown I*. The Governor of Arkansas, another Southern stalwart, eventually remarked that Arkansas would also obey the law. [17]

Federal government Reaction

President Eisenhower deployed his executive authority to desegregate the schools in the District of Columbia.[18] Of course, his authority was limited when it came to desegregation in states. In the Congress, the opposite result was the case, as over 110 members of the

Congress mostly from the South, authored the Southern Manifesto.[19] In so doing, this manifesto developed a strategy of delay and of nullification of the *Brown I* decision. [20]

Brown III

Linda Brown's involvement in the Court system's desegregation of public schools did not end in 1954. Instead, her fight continued, in the form of another Brown case, where in 1979, now at age 36, she agreed to reopen the case on behalf of her own children. [21] On July 29, 1994, Judge Richard Rodgers approved a new desegregation plan for Topeka Unified School District 501, and consequently closed the *Brown* case, almost 50 years after the NAACP first filed the case using Linda Brown's father Rev. Brown's name.[22]

Civil Rights Legacy of Brown

The *Brown I* and *II* cases had an indelible impact on the Civil Rights Movement, to say the least. At the outset, while Thurgood Marshall and the NAACP were dismantling the legal segregation in the Courts, Dr. Martin Luther King Jr., and the other civil rights activists were beginning to mobilize mass citizen protests and marches against the practical components of segregation. In fact, Thurgood's work began to overlap with Dr. King and the Southern Christian Leadership Conference's work in the South, in Birmingham, and Montgomery Alabama for instance. In fact, after *Brown II* was decided, in 1955, later that year, Ms. Rosa Parks sat down on a bus in Montgomery Alabama, and thereby sparked the modern Civil Rights Movement, with the Montgomery Bus Boycott. Then a few years later, four young men sat down at a lunch counter in Greensboro North Carolina. Thus, all across the South, there were sit-ins, boycotts, and other instances of civil disobedience. The victory in *Brown I*, was an important legal and moral victory for African Americans, and the modern Civil Rights Movement really began to increase and create momentum, all the way until the passage of the Civil Rights Act in 1964, and the Voting Rights Act in 1965, within a decade of the decision in *Brown II*.

Thus, the *Brown I* case sparked a glorious revolution for African Americans, and if the modern Civil Rights Movement is viewed from the perspective of a war, the *Brown I* case was a major victory in the battle against Jim Crow segregation. Moreover, the NAACP's victory in *Brown I* began to grow and develop that organization into the leading Civil Rights organization in that period, even after the separation of the Legal Defense Fund from the national organization, to get around IRS pressure. For Thurgood Marshall, the *Brown* cases were clearly the hallmark of his illustrious legal career; even despite his having help draft the constitution for country of Kenya, in Africa. However, Thurgood's legal career would not end there, he would go all the way to sitting as a Justice on the very court that he argued the *Brown* cases and others in front of for many years, until his health forced his retirement. The *Brown* cases clearly had a huge impact on his legal career and cemented his place as the greatest African American lawyer ever produced in America.

Legal Legacy of *Brown*

The *Brown* cases ushered in a new era for the U.S. Supreme Court as well as federal district courts across the United States. By virtue of the Court's decision in *Brown II*, federal district Court judges became the gatekeepers of school desegregation plans, as well as other cases involving civil rights. In this vein, the federal courts became a viable tool in the struggle for civil and human rights in this country. Thus, a cadre of federal judges, particularly in the South became stalwarts in forcing school systems to desegregate in order to comply with *Brown I* and *II*.

Furthermore, the Warren Court, would go on to decide many cases in the area of civil and human rights, including *Mapp v. Ohio* (1961) (establishing the exclusionary rule, preventing the prosecution from using evidence obtained in violation of the Fourth Amendment to the U.S. Constitution), *Gideon v. Wainwright* (1963) (establishing the right to a lawyer in a criminal case), *Miranda v. Arizona* (1966) (establishing the four warnings to be given for custodial interrogations: the right to remain silent, that anything said can and will be used against the accused in a court of law, that an accused has the right to an attorney, and that if one cannot afford an attorney, the government could provide one to them), and other cases which expanded the Bill of Rights and increased protections for citizens and their rights.[23] Moreover, Thurgood Marshall ushered in the role of the Civil Rights lawyer, many of whom, but not all, were African American. Thus, Julius Chambers in North Carolina would emerge as a preeminent civil rights lawyer in North Carolina, at one time, having approximately over 200 cases on the docket challenging discrimination or segregation in public education. Moreover, Attorney Chambers would go on to argue the *Swann v. Charlotte-Mecklenburg County Board of Education,* case, decided by the U.S. Supreme Court, as one of many children of the *Brown* cases.[24] In addition, in Alabama, such civil rights lawyers, as Oscar Adams, who would eventually become the first African American state supreme court justice in Alabama, U.W. Clemon, who would eventually become the first African-American federal judge in Alabama, J.L. Chesnut, J. Mason Davis, J. Richet Pearson, Fred Gray, who represented Ms. Parks, and many others would emerge.

In fact, Dr. King saw the need for an increase in African American lawyers, speaking to classes at Morehouse College, his alma mater, encouraging the young men to attend law school. Dr. King saw the success in *Brown I* and other cases, as well as the passage of the Civil and Voting Rights Acts. Dr. King admonished the young men that the movement was changing and that as these laws were being passed there would need to be lawyers who would step up and ensure that these laws were enforced, and if necessary, defended in the courts. Not only did *Brown I* help to usher in a generation of African American lawyers, but as a byproduct, there was also an increase in the number of African American jurists, both in federal and state courts, to include the Honorable Damon J. Keith, who rose to become the chief judge of the Sixth Circuit Court of Appeals in Michigan.

Educational Legacy of Brown

Although Charles Hamilton Houston, Thurgood Marshall, and others at the NAACP Legal Department, had already begun to dismantle segregation in higher education, the *Brown I* case, nonetheless continued that effort. More and more African Americans were admitted into areas of higher education like never before. This result produced what Dr. W.E.B. Dubois once called the talented tenth. A group of highly educated and skilled African Americans who could then lead the race out of the segregation of the past into the promise of tomorrow.

As for primary and secondary education, although *Brown I* did much for the principle of desegregation, it was limited in its practical result. These limitations were largely due to segregationist school systems and administrators so desperate to hold on to their dual system of education, that in some areas, the school systems simply shut down, rather than integrate. Moreover, it was during the time after *Brown I* and *II*, that many private or parochial schools began to appear and flourish across the country. With white families preferring to take their children out of the public-school systems in urban areas, through white flight, to live and have their children attend school in suburban areas. This was also a symptom of housing discrimination that was perpetuated in the U.S. for many decades during this time, with discriminatory housing association rules, and restrictive covenants in deeds, which were also eventually found unconstitutional by the U.S. Supreme Court.

In fact, it really was not until the passage of the 1964 Civil Rights Act, that public schools really saw an increase in desegregation, as President Johnson threatened to withhold federal funding for the schools if they did not desegregate in accordance with *Brown I*. This is perhaps one of the difficult legacies of *Brown I*. Over the years many scholars, activists, and others have debated about whether and to what extent *Brown I* helped the education of African Americans in this country. Indeed, by the 1990s, less than 50 years after Brown, public schools were almost more segregated than they were when *Brown I* was decided. While there are many sociological, societal, and other factors that likely caused this separation of the races in public schools, this was the reality, nonetheless. This phenomenon had people, even African American leaders casting some doubt as to the true benefit of *Brown I* to future generations of schoolchildren.

Moreover, there are startling statistics even today about the low performance of urban school systems mainly populated by African Americans, Latino Americans and other ethnic minorities. From reading deficiencies to high dropout rates, and low performance on standardized testing, there exists a great divide in the area of educational achievement between African Americans and White Americans. Some attribute these statistics to limited resources that teachers and administrators have with educational budgets getting even more strained year after year. Others blame DuBois' talented tenth, arguing that as African Americans gained more access to the upper echelon of society, they prospered, and somehow left the most vulnerable of the community behind. Still others blame institutional racism which has created a system which disfavors inner city youth who have less exposure to society and the world and does not account for the cultural differences that shaped these young lives. Some have argued that it was not enough to remove de jure or legal segregation, but that more should have been done to help students not just be able to attend the same schools but be able to enhance their educational journey. Nevertheless, the result of this debate may continue, and may never be resolved, but the fact is that whatever the current state of public education for African Americans, it is likely a far cry better than being labeled with a badge or inferiority, as a result of the separate education that Linda Brown was subjected to at the time of the *Brown I* case.

Another Brown

It is difficult if not impossible to find a Supreme Court case since *Brown I* that has equaled the impact this case had on the country. There have been cases involving such topics as abortion, gay marriage, and healthcare for all. In fact, in looking at the Court since *Brown I*, it has in many ways gone in the opposite direction of *Brown I*. Since *Brown I* the Court has arguably issued more decisions that have been considered pro-business and anti-union than ever before. In fact, the Court has been criticized in recent years as merely serving as an extension of the political arm at the time, whether conservative or liberal. Many of its decisions have fallen squarely along party lines, without any real ideological shift or surprise. The closest that the Court has come in more recent years to *Brown I*, is perhaps in the cases dealing with affirmative action. With a myriad of decisions, the Court has all but eradicated affirmative action in contracting, and severely limited its application in other areas including higher education.[25]

The Court has stopped short of getting rid of affirmative action altogether, but that does not mean that it will last forever. With the advent of a more partisan Congress and U.S. Supreme Court vacancies becoming more and more contentious in recent years, it is any wonder if the Court will ever have occasion to hear or let alone decide a case with the significance of *Brown I* soon. In fact, it is possible, that the Court may indeed fade into obscurity in the minds of many Americans given its relatively uncontroversial decisions in recent years. At a time, when depending upon the issue one can almost predict the outcome of the case and the vote of the justices based on their ideological backgrounds, it is likely that the Supreme Court may have lost its luster. Indeed, it is yet to be seen if the Roberts' Court or its successor Courts will ever take the Supreme Court back to the prominence that it once had around the time of the *Brown I* case. One can hope though, that the Court will carry out its constitutional duties in such a way to be the arbiter of the Constitution that former Chief Justice John Marshall once declared.

Brown I's Legacy in Twenty-First Century Society

The impact of *Brown I*, can still be felt in twenty-first century society, although in a slightly different way. The majority view of *Brown I* and likely the consensus is that it was rightly decided. But public education since *Brown I*, has undergone a strange transformation. Public schools are underfunded, in many ways due to the creation of charter and private schools, which educate students once forced to attend public schools, and in so doing, the funding of the schools has decreased significantly. This has left teachers overworked and underpaid, as well as students in many ways more segregated that at the time of *Brown I*. Through gentrification, neighborhoods have become even less diverse than before, and economic inequality have all contributed to the rise of poverty and lack of education in urban African American neighborhoods. All these phenomena created a conundrum for public education and as a result calls into consideration the value of *Brown I* today. Perhaps its value today is not just in the education context. No, *Brown I* went further than that; it spoke to the very heart of human decency and race relations, as well as to the ideals which this country has and purports to have at its core. *Brown, I* speaks to future generations to remind us of how far African Americans have come and indeed how far this country has come in terms of rising above hatred, racism, and white supremacy. But at the same time, it reminds us that these negative things may still exist, and when they do rear their ugly heads, *Brown I* stands as a shining example of how to deal with them at least before the law.

Brown I likely represents different things to different people. To African Americans, *Brown I* is a watershed moment, it is a time when African Americans triumphed in the highest court in the land and were able to obtain for themselves a victory which only a few years earlier seemed unattainable. To whites, and others, and even African Americans, *Brown I* reminds us of the danger of separating races, and generalizing groups of people based on no more information than their skin color. In a post-*Brown I* era it is possible that such generalizations may manifest themselves not just by race, but by religion, by country of origin, or other general classifications of people. *Brown I* reminds us of the past that we must remember and learn from in order to grow and face the challenges of society in the future.

Enduring Legacy of Brown I

Brown I sparked the dawn of a new age in American race relations. In terms of history, this case should take its place in the library of African American historical events which eventually changed the destiny of African Americans in this country. *Brown I* is more than just a Supreme Court case. It is more than just the five cases which were consolidated by the Court. It is about much more than just the nine men, who decided the case. It is about more than just the learned counsel on either side of the case. It is about more than just the NAACP. It is about more than just *Plessy v. Ferguson*, even though that was one of the main issues in the case. *Brown I* was a beacon of light at the end of a very dark tunnel. The tunnel which began with the most brutal, violent, and inhumane peculiar institution of slavery, that then traveled through Reconstruction briefly, then through Jim Crow segregation, and finally to rise to the mountaintop of dismantling segregation in post-secondary, and eventually primary and secondary education.

Just like the case itself, *Brown I* has a complicated legacy. It is an amalgam of emotions, contradictions, and criticisms. In particular, one of the great debates regarding *Brown I*, is the counterargument, the Washingtonian query of whether *Brown I* may have hurt African Americans in terms of focusing on integration to perhaps the exclusion of self-reliance. The basis of this argument is that when African Americans were relegated to their own schools, being taught by their own teachers, and being surrounded by their own intellectuals, they gained invaluable experiences, insight, and collective thought. The argument continues that after *Brown I*, integration separated these institutions, and consequently extracted the brightest of the bright out of African American institutions into majority institutions. By doing so many African Americans suffered as they were being taught in white schools by white teachers, who may not have the same interest and motivation for educating African American students as African American teachers had.

In addition, this argument continues that that by opening up the academy and other places where Dr. Dubois' talented tenth could ascend, *Brown I* separated African American people between those who had the ability and education to rise out of poverty and those who were left behind. Moreover, HBCUs produced some of the greatest talent in African American history, but years later many of them struggle for survival, after integration and *Brown I*. These counterarguments may not be successful, but it is difficult to discuss the issue of *Brown I*, and integration without having these points raised. There are those who would raise the question about how much *Brown I* helped African American education vs. African Americans in general. For instance, *Brown I* raised the caliber for African Americans as a people in many sectors of society, but it may not have had the same affect in education. Moreover, as discussed earlier, the *Brown I* case itself, did not necessarily literally force all school doors open in all primary and secondary schools. To the contrary the case itself, paved the way for the school doors to open, but it was not the key that unlocked the door to integration of public schools. Instead, that remedy had to come from another branch of government, which resulted from a different kind of fight. This goes back to something Dr. King once wrote about the utility of using litigation as a tool for broad social change. It is in this context that an analysis of *Brown I* can be keenly observed. *Brown I* was a court case, with parties, lawyers, and judges. The very fact that it involved the legal system, placed arbitrary limitations on its reach.

Dr. King pointed out that what mass protest could do, sometimes litigation could not do. He described how in many instances, litigation relegates the people involved to passive observers, rather than active participants. This is because the legal system in and of itself is limited as a means of producing change. The success, although short-lived of the efforts by those in the South and elsewhere in either delaying or preventing integration, are proof of the limitation that sometimes litigation poses to accomplishing an end.

One of the chief criticisms of *Brown I* then, is the viability of using courts to address social issues and problems. Even today, litigation is costly, lengthy, very tedious, and usually takes an immeasurable toll on all parties involved. In fact, in many cases, like in *Brown I* and *Brown II*, any victory is short-lived or otherwise loses its luster due to the limitations placed upon it by the court or the law. Nevertheless, despite its limitations, litigation can be an effective tool to spark further action to achieve change. *Brown I* was an important moment, and it forced the issue of segregation squarely at the seat of government. It is likely that when the Congress passed and the President signed the Civil Rights Act of 1964 and the Voting Rights Act of 1965, they had *Brown I* in their rearview mirror. The fact that one of the three co-equal branches of the federal government had already spoken loudly through *Brown I* on the issue of segregation likely affected the other two branches of government. But not only that, the victory in *Brown I* likely energized those marchers and protesters who continued their fight to desegregate restaurants, hotels, and other places of public accommodations leading to the groundswell of support for the Civil and Voting Rights Acts.

Brown I was a long and hard-fought battle that began some 20 years before the case was decided. It was a battle of wills, of endurance, of setbacks of victories, and ultimately the pinnacle of victory in *Brown I*, and somber defeat in *Brown II*. Yet, when the other families in Topeka began the case which Rev. Oliver Brown eventually joined, they likely could not have imagined that the case would have garnered the attention that it did. It is likely that they were not thinking about sparking a generation of civil rights activism and change. It is more likely that these parents and Rev. Brown, like all parents, were concerned about their children, having the opportunity to attend a quality school that was convenient to their neighborhood. They were concerned with their children not being prohibited from attending a school that their white friends could attend simply because of their race. Rev. Brown and the other families in Topeka achieved that victory. When Linda Brown attended 7th grade at an integrated junior high school, she, her father, and her entire family experienced a triumphant victory over segregation and oppression. It is not clear if Rev. Brown ever grasped the full meaning and value that his fight achieved, and what his case would mean to generations to come. But it was not lost on his daughter. Linda knew the weight of her father's fight and the case that bears her name.

Linda Brown passed away in 2018, after having continued the fight her father started, almost over half a century earlier. She dedicated her life to desegregation and everything her father and her case stood for. An organization was created to continue to highlight and preserve her historic case. In this way, African Americans and indeed all Americans and others can observe and celebrate the courage, will, and perseverance that she, her father, the other families, the NAACP, and so many others displayed on their way to this monumental victory.

―――― CHAPTER 10 ――――

LESSONS FROM MOVEMENT MENTORS

A LL THREE OF THESE men, Dred Scott, Homer Plessy, and Rev. Oliver Brown are Movement Mentors and offer lessons for current and future activists. Although occurring at different times, and in different eras, their cases and struggles had common threads that may be useful to those committed to civil rights activism and social change today. This chapter will pull together common themes from the lives and cases of these men who were all triumphant, even if at the time their victory may have seemed hollow, afar off, or even non-existent.

Lesson 1: Defeat as a doorway to victory

One of the first lessons from our Movement Mentors, is that losing is not always a permanent fate. Instead, sometimes losing one battle reveals the keys to victory for future battles and eventually to the war. The *Dred Scott* case personifies this. He lost in what most would consider a resounding fashion. Only two Justices dissented. Moreover, despite the contrary positions of some scholars, Dred Scott's case truly laid the groundwork and set the stage for what soon became inevitable, Civil War, and Reconstruction. *Dred Scott* forced the federal government and the nation to confront something that up until that time had been mostly ignored and shunned: Slavery was an evil institution that was condoned by the federal government.

Moreover, it proved that slavery had to be dealt with in a meaningful way. It showed that this country would have to deal with its treatment of the African people and their descendants one way or another. Chief Justice Taney, who issued the infamous majority opinion in *Dred Scott,* indicated that people of African descent had no rights which the white man was bound by law to respect. Such a broad statement, echoes forth even today.This is a startling statement by the chief judicial official in the United States. As such, the case created a large imprint on the dashboard of the country and was a very important factor in the election of 1860. This election produced a President and a Congressional majority willing to finally confront this issue, unlike their predecessors, who ignored the issue for so long.

Dred Scott forever changed the course of this country's history, all because of one unassuming laborer, his wife, a laundress, and their family. Dred Scott, this ordinary person, did something extraordinary. In truth Dred Scott was not the only person to sue for his freedom, but his case was unique in that rather than hide behind legal technicalities, differing interpretations, or laws passed by different states, it forced the issue. Dred Scott's case called into question the very heart of the matter: Was slavery truly the intent of the federal government from the beginning? Was it a stain on this nation that would never go away? Dred Scott's case gave the Supreme Court the opportunity to answer these questions with dignity and morality.

Unfortunately, the Court chose to do the opposite. Instead, it chose to further mar and denigrate enslaved people of African ancestry. *Dred Scott* provides the answer to why one race treats others of a different race so drastically different. With hate groups rising around the country and the world, Dred Scott's case is a sobering reminder of what can happen when the institutions that were formed purportedly to protect the rights of all, only protect the rights of a privileged (white) few. *Dred Scott* is an example of what occurs when those with the power to change society, hide behind its prejudices and ill-advised traditions, rather than confront them.

Dred's Scott's case is about more than winning or losing. Ultimately, Dred Scott did win his freedom, not through the courts, but by changing the hearts and minds of the Blow family. The *Dred Scott* case forced many people to reconsider their position on slavery, and in doing so, Dred was victorious. Moreover, he was even more victorious when the rights which he fought to obtain were granted to African Americans a little over 10 years after his case ended in defeat. Those rights, embodied in the 13th 14th and 15th Amendments of the U.S. Constitution will stand forever, and protect not only African Americans but all Americans. Thus, Dred's loss eventually became the key to victory, and this is his true legacy.

But Dred, is not the only Movement Mentor to display this important principle. Homer Plessy also displayed it, with his courageous challenge to the Louisiana Separate Car Law almost 50 years after Dred's case. In fact, it is logical to conclude that *Plessy v. Ferguson* grew out of *Dred Scott v. Sandford*. Like Dred, Homer Plessy lost his case. Homer's defeat, however, was even more damaging that Dred's. Whereas Dred Scott was a set-up for a come-back in the form of Reconstruction, Plessy ended up being a set-back in the form of Jim Crow segregation which saw an increase in the lynching and other senseless killings of thousands of African Americans.[1]

Jim Crow Segregation was as close to slavery as any condition. The Supreme Court's decision in Homer Plessy's case emboldened the Ku Klux Klan, and other domestic terrorists who sought to relegate African Americans to as near as the property that Chief Justice Taney declared their ancestors were in the *Dred Scott* decision. According to later civil rights lawyers and activists, Homer Plessy's loss greatly set back the struggle for freedom and equality in this country.

Nevertheless, Homer Plessy's case gave future civil rights lawyers the keys to its own demise, in the *Brown I* case. The separate but equal pronouncement in *Plessy* was the strategy that Charles Hamilton Houston and later, Thurgood Marshall ultimately used to undo it. Thus, *Plessy* gave them a target to aim for, and with their strategic thinking, masterful preparation, and dogged determination, they were able to use that target and eventually bring it to its knees. There have been some who argued that if there was no *Plessy v. Ferguson* decision, there may have been no need for the *Brown v. Board of Education I* decision. However, one thing is abundantly clear, if there were no loss in *Plessy*, there would have been no victory in *Brown I*. If *Dred Scott* and even *Plessy* are the greatest defeats for African Americans and those that fight for equal rights for all races, then *Brown v. Board of Education I* may have been the greatest victory. An important lesson then for current and future activists is that even though they may and likely will suffer losses in court, in attempting to pass legislation, blocking a Supreme Court nominee, impeaching a President, or curtailing a rubber-stamping Congress, the fight is still worth having. An activist is just that, they fight the fights that need fighting. Even in defeat, an activist has victory, because they fought for a cause for which they truly believed in. An activist is not judged by their win-loss record. No, an activist is judged by their commitment to the fight, their courage to resist, and their determination to press forward until either a victory is one, or a loss which will eventually lead to a victory occurs.

Lesson 2: Dangers of a Stagnant Government

Another important lesson which can be gleaned from these Movement Mentors is that a stagnant government can be very dangerous to a society. Even prior to the *Dred Scott* case, it was the stagnation and inaction of the executive and legislative branches on the issue of slavery, which eventually led to the *Dred Scott* case.[2] Moreover, such inaction can be traced to some of the beginnings of the Civil War. At this country's founding, to paraphrase President Lincoln, it was a house was divided against itself, in the form of the enslavement of people of African descent. As such, Lincoln correctly noted, this house could not remain divided against itself and stand, without action to rebuild it.

Plessy v. Ferguson is no different. In the build-up to *Plessy*, the federal government acquiesced in the face of rising animosity by the states, that began passing laws designed to maintain segregation between African Americans and whites in several areas of society. Slowly, but surely the former Confederate States, began to enact legal barriers to full equality for African Americans, relegating this people to a second class or even worse, a return to the status of property. All the while the federal government stood idly by in some cases and emboldened states in others. The *Plessy* decision was a direct byproduct of such inaction. Although, *Plessy* only dealt with the Separate Car Law in Louisiana, the Supreme Court's decision was applied in nearly every industry, including education, public accommodations, and other contexts.

While some may not be able to tie *Plessy* directly to the rise of Jim Crow segregation, it was the key that segregationists had been looking for. Tacit approval by the highest court in the land that segregation was not only permitted but could be required in some cases. Moreover, prior to the *Brown I* decision, the Supreme Court took every opportunity not to decide the central issues raised in that case, as the Court distinguished previous cases on the facts on the one hand, or merely reserved the questions for later cases on the other. It wasn't until the NAACP lawyers made it unavoidable, that the Court finally squarely addressed the issue of segregation in public schools. In the meantime, African American students suffered under the weight of underfunded and substandard schools, with the attendant psychological and sociological effects of segregation from white students. The federal government's inaction directly affected the public education system, prior to *Brown I*. Even after *Brown I*, the Court's trepidation in immediately enforcing desegregation, by virtue of its decision in *Brown II*, helped to stifle integration in public schools for several years after the case was decided. In any event, the Court's predilection for inaction or slow action nevertheless set back the condition of African Americans for decades.

Lesson 3: Building Organizations lays the Foundation to a Movement

Another very important lesson from our Movement Mentors, is that becoming organized in action and forming organizations of like-minded people are key to making effective social change. In *Plessy*'s case, the Citizens Committee of New Orleans was very active and very disciplined in their challenge to Jim Crow segregation. They were also able to reach a broad coalition in order to fight against oppression and inequality. In the same way, the NAACP, formed not long after *Plessy* was decided, began its 20-year legal fight against segregation culminating in the *Brown I* decision. Thus, both *Plessy* and *Brown I* were the result of organizations of committed persons.

The NAACP organized various chapters to fight segregation on the ground in different states, and simultaneously created and funded a legal team dedicated to fighting segregation in the courts. This multi-pronged strategy proved to be magnificently successful, as the NAACP legal department and its successor, the NAACP Legal Defense and Education Fund (LDF), obtained significant legal victories over the years to combat, curtail, and cancel legalized segregation and discriminatory practices.

Moreover, the NAACP-LDF, produced generations of civil rights lawyers, judges, and other influential figures, to include the first African American Supreme Court justice. The victories of the NAACP and the NAACP-LDF are numerous and the accolades are well-deserved. However, one of the areas that gets minimal attention is the importance of the fact that these organizations have been sustained for many years, and in the case of the NAACP, for over a century. Thus, to other benefits of having organizations are longevity, and continuity that spans multiple generations of leaders and activists. By creating an organization of dedicated people, the NAACP made it difficult to silence many voices instead of only a few or one. In addition, having an organization provides structure to activism, a sense of history, purpose, and a consistent vision and mission for the members of the organization to follow. Synergy among members has been crucial in terms of success both inside and outside the legal system. These previous activists did not have tools and resources such as the internet and social media, like activists have today, but their organizations allowed them to be successful, nonetheless.

Thus, the tool of creating organizations of like-minded individuals, or building a tribe is imperative for current and future activists to not only create change, but a social movement that will have long-lasting affects and impacts for generations to come. Organizations can stand the test of time. Many of the most prominent feats that have changed the way we do and see things, are due to the success of organizations. Even when the people changed, the organizations remained. Moreover, many Modern Civil Rights Movement leaders who made a tremendous impact and created social change, did so while creating organizations.

For instance, Dr. King and Rev. Abernathy were part of the Southern Christian Leadership Conference ("SCLC"). Thurgood Marshall had the NAACP, and later the NAACP-LDF. Tourgée and Homer Plessy worked with the New Orleans Citizens Committee. In addition, Dred Scott had several lawyers throughout his case, his wife, who also filed a legal challenge, and several benefactors, including the Blow family who provided financial backing for his case, and eventually granted him his freedom. Thus, Dred Scott's pursuit of his freedom was the result of a group of people who shared his vision for freedom, and who actively participated in bringing about that result. That is what the definition of an organization is.

In Rev. Oliver Brown's case, as a minister he was already part of a large Christian organization, a member of the African Methodist Episcopal (AME) Church, and an associate pastor of his local church. Thus, Rev. Brown also believed in joining organizations that he could participate in. Not only that, but Rev. Brown also joined twelve other families who decided to challenge the segregated school system in Topeka, Kansas. It is interesting that when he and the other parents tried to enroll their children in the all-white schools individually, their efforts were unsuccessful. However, when they joined together, and with the NAACP legal team in challenging the segregated school system in Topeka Kansas, they met with different results, this time a victorious outcome.

Taken even further, the *Brown I* and *II* cases were not comprised of just one case, as indicated earlier in the book, but these cases each were consolidated across four states and the District of Columbia, for the purpose of deciding them. Moreover, these cases came from states in the South, the Midwest, the North, and even a non-state, the District of Columbia. It is not a misstatement to say that if the cases had only come from say Virginia, or South Carolina, that it could have had an impact on the Court and possibly the outcome of the cases. In fact, members of the Court clearly had thoughts about the necessity of consolidating the cases, and those considerations factored into Kansas being the lead case among the group of five cases. Thus, even the cases themselves were submitted and considered as a part of an organization of cases coming before the Supreme Court.

Furthermore, the importance of organizing and building something to last, was not lost on the minor child of Rev. Brown, Linda, in that she not only continued the fight against segregated schools as an adult for her own child, but a foundation was formed dedicated to the *Brown I* case, and its history.[3] Thus, it appears that these three courageous men and those that worked with them understood the power of organizations, and how they are an integral part of making social change and building a civil rights movement in any age.

Lesson 4: Building Wide Coalitions Creates Shared Vision

Another very important lesson that these men teach us is the importance of building wide coalitions to assist in any movement for social change. Each of these men were able to develop wide coalitions across different groups of people who had a common interest in the work that each man attempted to accomplish. For instance, Homer Plessy, and the Citizen's Committee in New Orleans not only already had a broad coalition within their ranks but they were also able to enlist the railroad company in their effort to challenge the Separate

Car Law in Louisiana and desegregate railcars. In fact, the railroad company's support of Plessy in this fight was due largely to the cost that having extra cars would place on the railroad. Thus, the Railroad company's interests converged with that of Homer Plessy and the Citizens Committee. This is a very early historical example of the interest convergence theory developed and advanced by the late great Law Professor Derrick Bell, to whom the Critical Race Theory owes part of its creation, and many theories concerning race and the law.[4] This idea is rooted in the fact that although various groups may have different interests there may be common interests that are aligned for one reason or another and to the extent that activists can find that common interest with other groups, there is the opportunity to build a coalition around the common interests thereby increasing the strength and likelihood that each group accomplishes their stated goals.

In addition, in the *Dred Scott* case, the person listed as the defendant in his case, Sanford, who was the relative of Dr. Emerson's wife to whom Dred and Harriett had been sold, acquiesced in becoming the defendant in the case, in order to allow federal jurisdiction to be obtained to have the case filed in federal court.

Furthermore, in the *Brown I* case, the NAACP used a wide coalition of lawyers and others in support of their efforts. The renowned historian, Dr. John Hope Franklin helped the NAACP lawyers as they researched the circumstances surrounding the passage of the 14th Amendment and its equal protection clause, while answering the questions posed by the Court for re-argument.[5] Furthermore, Dr. Kenneth Clark and his wife assisted the NAACP with providing anecdotal evidence regarding the effect of segregation on Negro children, in a study that was ultimately cited in the *Brown I* decision.[6] Thus, a broad coalition of people and forces aided in pursuing and bringing about the decision in *Brown I*.

In terms of putting together a coalition to support social change, it is imperative for current and future activists to be coalition builders. Even during the abolitionist movement Fredrick Douglas, William Lloyd Garrison, and others, were able to put together coalition of abolitionists, people fighting for women's suffrage, and others in order to bring about change. Their efforts along with *Dred Scott*, resulted in the issuance of the Emancipation Proclamation, and later passage of the 13th Amendment abolishing slavery.

During the modern Civil Rights Movement in this country, Dr. King and other civil rights leaders joined with actors, such as Harry Belafonte, writers like James Baldwin, other religious and other kinds of groups, and people of different races and religious backgrounds, to fight against Jim Crow segregation. There are countless examples where activists were able to unite across political, social, racial, gender and other lines in order to achieve a common worthwhile goal.

Lesson 5: Legal Remedies are Just One Tool in the Toolbox

Although alluded to throughout the book, and referred to directly in some places, litigation as a form of social change has its advantages and its disadvantages. In general, litigation by its very nature is expensive, time-consuming, and the parties lack control over its outcome. These disadvantages are even greater in the case of social justice litigation. Additionally, the judges in civil rights cases are not as sensitive to, nor familiar with the subjects of the activism. While this is not always the case, the need for litigation evidences the lack of settled law or vice versa favoring the cause of the social justice lawyering. Consequently, social justice litigation tends to require the plaintiffs to change the mind of a judge, or jury, or panel of judges, that the status quo is not correct, and instead rule that a new law or rule should be established.

Furthermore, as the men in this book and their cases illustrate, no matter what direction the wheels of justice turn, they most certainly turn slowly. This should be abundantly clear from the first two men's experiences in this book, as they both lost their cases, in dramatic fashion. In fact, it took almost 100 years for the law of the land to go from African Americans having no rights that a white man was bound to respect, to segregation is inherently unequal. Thus, social justice lawyering is indeed playing the long game. Nevertheless, as indicated earlier there is some value in using litigation as a tool. For instance, litigation helps to frame the issue that a group, organization, or movement is attempting to change. In addition, litigation helps to articulate the importance and the necessity of the issue at hand, not only for the court, but also for the public at large. Furthermore, litigation can generate a certain degree of publicity and even garner support from others who follow the case closely. Indeed, the *Brown I* case is proof of the power of a successful litigation effort.

On the other hand, *Brown II*, effectively demonstrates the limitations of a victory in litigation. Many times, a decision is limited to its facts, or even worse, the remedy can sometimes become a barrier or obstacle to the right sought to be protected. This makes clear what Dr. King and others likely always knew, which is that litigation is an effective tool in the toolbox of civil rights and social justice activism, but it is merely one tool to be used in addition to, rather than instead of, other tools. It is likely that by spurring the passage of the 1964 Civil Rights Act, marching feet in 1963 in the March on Washington, did more to advance the cause of school integration, than the *Brown I* decision did in and of itself.[7]

This is not to say that *Brown II* rendered *Brown I* completely toothless. But as *Brown I* proved, a case won in court sometimes must be continuously revisited for years to ensure compliance with the decision. Moreover, Courts are not designed for, nor should they be, a place for unelected judges (at least at the federal level) to decide a course of action. In addition, the current political environment, the increasing conservatism in the judiciary, and the role of money and multi-national corporations in the political and legal system, further exacerbate the problems posed by litigation as a tool. This will undoubtedly make social activist litigation much more difficult to prevail in court, as time goes on. Thus, the stories, events, and cases in this book involving these three men teach current and future activists that while litigation should remain apart of their overall strategy, it must be joined with other strategies that provide for the inclusion of large numbers of followers to bring about social change.

Lesson 6: Mass Resistance is Effective

Speaking of additional strategies in the toolbox, mass resistance is still an effective tool to bring about social change. If there are any failings in these cases, with these three extraordinary men, it is that there was not a great mass movement or protest behind them. Despite the existence of a broad coalition or at least several people working and fighting on their behalf, there was not the great mass resistance, such as the Civil Rights Movement of the 1950's and 1960's that would eventually follow the last case discussed in this book. In Dred's Scott's case, the closest thing to mass resistance, in an albeit more violent and destructive manner, was the raid on Harper's Ferry by John Brown and his followers. This attack certainly instilled fear and trepidation in the hearts of those who perpetuated the institution of slavery, but it was futile in its efforts, and only resulted in tremendous loss of life, no matter how noble the purported purpose was.

Ultimately Brown and his followers were captured, tried, and executed for their activities. This underscores the importance of civil non-violent disobedience and protest, like that Dr. King and others, including Mahatma Gandhi before him, preached and practiced. A mass movement of African Americans or white supporters attempting to free Dred Scott by force would have done little for his case. It would have allowed the opponents of Dred's case to argue for the savageness of African Americans and could have been used a justification for denying him and his wife the relief they ultimately sought. A mass civil demonstration on the other hand, particularly on the courthouse steps and even in the halls of Congress could have had some effect on those involved in the case. Particularly at that time, if there was visible support from whites, it might have gone a long way to at least change the narrative that was being propagated during the time of the *Dred Scott* case.

In Homer Plessy's case, he had Tourgée and the Citizens Committee behind him, and although they engaged in litigation challenging segregation in many areas of life, it is not clear how much mass resistance played a role in their form of resistance. In fact, it is likely that the Citizens' Committee themselves and certainly Tourgée favored legal relief, in the place of mass civil resistance. Even fast forward to *Brown I* and *Brown II*, certainly civil disobedience had begun to be used or soon would be used immediately after the cases were decided. But it was really the next year, after *Brown I* was decided, the same year the *Brown II* decision was issued, and Emmett Till was murdered, that an unassuming lady in Montgomery, Alabama began what would become one of the greatest acts of civil disobedience. By remaining in her seat on a segregated bus, Mrs. Rosa Parks' act and arrest, eventually led to the Montgomery

Bus Boycott, one of the most successful early campaigns of massive resistance that sparked the modern Civil Rights movement.

This protest led to desegregation of the buses in Montgomery, and eventually albeit more slowly, a decision by the U.S. Supreme Court outlawing segregation on buses.[8] But it was not only Mrs. Parks in 1955, but five years later it was a group of students in Greensboro North Carolina, at a Woolworth's lunch counter, then it was a protest in Nashville, Tennessee, then the freedom rides throughout the South. Before long, like a wildfire, mass resistance sprang up all over the South and the rest of the country, like a cleverly planned military campaign. These protests would spark resistance from authorities, arrest, incarceration, and then later overturning of the laws being protested. Then a penultimate protest brought thousands from across the country to the nation's capital to hear a young preacher from Atlanta, talk about his dream. This massive protest, which was organized in part by arguably two preeminent leaders on mass organization for African Americans, A. Philip Randolph, and Bayard Rustin.

Over the objections of both President Kennedy and his brother, Attorney General Robert Kennedy, Dr. King and civil rights leaders pressed forward, and the March on Washington for Jobs and Freedom took place on August 28, 1963. Today a monument stands to not only commemorate Dr. King's life, but as a powerful reminder of the success that can come with mass resistance and protests. Another reason why mass protests are a useful tool, is that it allows everyday people to participate and bring about social change. Everyone will not be the great orator that Dr. King was, nor the great lawyer, and later Judge and Supreme Court Justice, that Thurgood Marshall was. Nor will everyone win gold medals and break records like Jesse Owens, Wilma Rudolph, or Ralph Boston. Everyone will not create a business empire like A.G. Gaston in Birmingham, the Spauldings of North Carolina, or Oprah Winfrey. But everyone can use their voice and their limbs as they have them to fight for social justice and change. That is the genius of mass protests: all can be apart.

Moreover, while Dred, Homer, and Rev. Brown, were individuals in their respective times, having mass protests ensure that the opposition cannot silence one individual or a few individuals in hopes of stifling the movement for social change. Instead, when one is arrested, ten more come to take their place, until so many people are arrested or jailed, that the jails are full. At that point, the powers that be must decide to change the laws, or be forced to incur significant hours, personnel, and resources due to a mass protest of individuals. In this way, the examples set by these men show current and future generations that mass protest must be a major part of activism and the push for social change. In addition, with the advent of social media and the internet, mass resistance should be easier, as the message and plans of resistance can now be broadcast over a wide range of mediums and even around the world in some cases merely with the push of a button or the click of a link. Such organizations as Black Lives Matter and Color of Change, have demonstrated this idea. Thus, current, and future activists are well advised to heed this lesson, and build movements that will include and involve mass resistance and protests in a large way.

Lesson 7: Movements Require Sacrifice

It is fitting, to end where this book began, especially given that this chapter is about lessons we can learn from these three Movement Mentors. Probably the most important of the lessons in this chapter, and themes throughout this book is the sacrifice that is required for a movement. As mentioned in the introduction to this book, the late great political scientist, historian, and activist, Dr. Ron Walters, was known for saying the difference between a movement and a moment, is sacrifice. His words are well taken and are evidenced by the experiences of these three men. Dred Scott, Harriet Scott, and the entire Scott family endured great cost, personally, emotionally, and even physically in order to continue their fight all the way to the U.S. Supreme Court. Their entire family was affected by their decision to make a stand and attempt to obtain their freedom, and at least attempt to put an end to the peculiar institution of slavery. Dred and Harriett lost their case, and the toll that it took on their family is likely immeasurable. Their case spanned many years, many lawyers, and many rulings. All the while they remained in limbo or in the charge or custody officially of the sheriff of St. Louis County, Missouri, until their fate was decided. This was their cost, and the price they had to pay in order to seek change and ultimately their freedom.

Similarly Homer Plessy and the Citizens Committee, suffered great pains and sacrifice to bring about the *Plessy* decision that would likely haunt them, and to a large extent many African Americans, and their descendants for years to come, with the rise of Jim Crow segregation. What Homer Plessy and the Citizens Committee likely thought would be a watershed moment in the area of Civil Rights, instead became their greatest defeat. Not to be overwhelmed, they continued their fight, but the opposition had ammunition in the form of the *Plessy* decision. Increasingly new slates of segregationist law after segregationist law would plague African Americans for a generation. Their costs were high, as they sacrificed, time, money, energy, and even a setback of previous gains made in the area of desegregation.

In the case of Rev. Brown, and many of the other parents of children involved in the *Brown I* case, there was also sacrifice, negative attention locally and nationally, as well as the risk that would be involved. During this time, if families from a community wanted the

NAACP's legal help, as a prerequisite, they would have to commit to bringing a direct legal challenge in the courts. Of course, this caused Rev. Brown and the other families to endure the risk of costly and protracted litigation over several years, involving multiple hearings at the lower court level, and even three arguments, and two decisions by the U.S. Supreme Court over the span of a couple of years to bring about their case's resolution. When Linda Brown recalled her father's excitement upon hearing of the decision in the case, it is likely that he thought back to all the time, effort, resources, and energy he and his family had expended and sacrificed in pursuit of this result. Only to finally have the result occur in their favor. The Brown family had three generations affected by their cases, from Rev. Brown, to Linda, to Linda's son. This evidences the cost and sacrifice that was necessitated by their family's decision to bring their case and take a stand. In each of these cases, there were moments, but these moments were transformed to movements by the willingness of these men, their families, and others who supported them to make the sacrifices necessary to bring about change, no matter how long it ultimately took to produce the desired result.

Conclusion

All three of these Movement Mentors call out to current and future generations through the conduit of history in order to provide context to their struggle and to encourage activists to continue seeking social justice and protecting civil rights. The fact that these men brought their cases in the times in which they did, helps to illuminate a path for future activists to follow. Almost like the proverbial breadcrumbs from fabled stories, these men and their cases light the path toward freedom, equality, and social change. Moreover, they illustrate in a very clear context, the continued need for movements, and struggle for social change. Despite the fact each in their own way achieved some level of success, after a time, there would arise a new challenge or obstacle, requiring a new movement to be perpetuated and promulgated by people as motivated and determined as they were.

While these men are forever etched in the historical and indeed legal fabric of the American story, their cases are but peaks of deep mountains of activism that have permeated throughout time. They continue to speak to us and illustrate how courage and determination are necessary ingredients for any person who will answer the call of justice to make a positive change for themselves and society. Dred Scott, Homer Plessy, and Rev. Oliver Brown, evidence how an enslaved person, a cobbler, and an AME preacher, respectively, became household names in the U.S. Supreme Court, the highest court in the land. Each one has been and will continue to be studied by generations of legal scholars, historians, lawyers, judges, and even schoolchildren. Across the span of time, they provide inspiration, motivation, and encouragement as our Movement Mentors.

END

NOTES

Introduction: Movements Require Sacrifice

1 Dr. Ron Walters (July 20, 1938 – September 10, 2010), former chair and professor of political science at Howard University and Syracuse University, assistant professor and chair of African American Studies at Brandeis University, and visiting professor at Princeton University.

2 Frederick Douglass, "Two Speeches by Frederick Douglass; West India Emancipation.. And the Dred Scott Decision," *C. P. Dewey, Manuscript/Mixed Material.* Retrieved January 20, 2020, from Library of Congress. https://www.loc.gov/item/mfd.21039/.August 4, 1857.

3 Dr. Martin Luther King, Jr., "Remaining Awake Through a Great Revolution," (speech, National Cathedral, Washington, D.C., March 31,1968, Congressional Record, April 9, 1968), The Martin Luther King, Jr., Research and Education Institute, Stanford University, Apri 27, 2020, https://kinginstitute.stanford.edu/king-papers/publications/knock-midnight-inspiration-great-sermons-reverend-martin-luther-king-jr-10.

4 Barack H. Obama, "In Commemorative MLK Speech, President Obama Recalls His Own 2008 Dream." *Swampland Time.* August 28, 2013. Retrieved January 20, 2020 from

https://swampland.time.com/2013/08/28/in-commemorative-mlk-speech-president-obama-recalls-his-own-2008-dream/.

5   Earl M. Maltz. *Dred Scott and the Politics of Slavery* (Lawrence: University Press of Kansas, 2007), vii.

Notes to Chapter 1: To Ask The Unthinkable

1   Stephen Faleski, "Local historical markers listed in 'Virginia History Trails.'" *The Tidewater News*. (The Virginia State Historical Marker tells us, the journey's hero, "a slave, lived as a child northeast of here on the Peter Blow Plantation early in the 1800's..."). February 8, 2019. https://www.thetidewaternews.com/2019/02/08/local-historical-markers-listed-in-virginia-history-trails/.

2   Kenneth M. Stampp. *The Peculiar Institution.* (New York: Alfred A. Knof, Inc. and Vintage Books, A Division of Random House, Inc., 1956), 24.

3   Stampp, *Peculiar Institution*, 32.

4   Ibid.

5   Stampp, *Peculiar Institution*, 48

6   Maltz, *Politics of Slavery*, 60.

7   Ibid;Faleski, *Local historical markers*

8   Allen, Austin. *Origins of the Dred Scott case: Jacksonian jurisprudence and the Supreme Court, 1837-1857.* (Athens: University of Georgia Press, 2006), 140-141

9   Maltz, *Politics of Slavery*, 60

10   Allen, *Origins of the Dred Scott case*, 141

11   Ibid.

12   Maltz, *Politics of Slavery*, 62

13   Ibid.

14   Allen, *Origins of the Dred Scott case*, 142

15   Maltz, *Politics of Slavery*, 61

16 Ibid.
17 Allen, *Origins of the Dred Scott case*, 140-141.
18 Ibid, 203, 219 (Reactions to the decision in the *Dred Scott* case were mixed in the media, along party lines, with pro-slavery Democrats lauding the decision, while anti-slavery Republicans calling for the decision to be overturned and slavery ended in the territories of the country).
19 Ibid, 140-141.
20 Maltz, *Politics of Slavery*, 140 (The Scotts were transferred to Taylor Blow, Peter Blow's son, and immediately freed in May 1857.)
21 Benjamin Disraeli, "*Quotes.*" *Optimize*. Retrieved on January 7, 2020. https://www.optimize.me/quotes/benjamin-disraeli/259039-nothing-can-resist-a-human-will-that-will-stake-its.
22 United States v. Schooner Amistad, 40 U.S. 518 (1841) (Held that the captured Africans should not be returned to those who captured them, but instead retained their freedom.); Prigg v. Pennsylvania, 41 U.S. 539 (1842)(Held that the Pennsylvania law that prevented extradition of enslaved persons to other states was unconstitutional and violated the Fugitive Slave Act of 1793.); Maltz, *Politics of Slavery*, 25-33.
23 John Hope Franklin. *From Slavery to Freedom*, Eighth ed. (New York: Alfred A. Knopf, a Division of Random House of Canada Ltd., 2000), 150-151 (For instance, 98 enslaved persons performed labor at the Saluda factory located in South Carolina, while an enslaved engineer worked on the West Feliciana Railroad).
24 Thomas Jefferson, et al, "Declaration of Independence." July 4, 1776.
25 Dred Scott v. Sandford, 60 U.S. 393 (1857).

Notes to Chapter 2: *Dred Scott, An Infamous Case*

1. Marbury v. Madison, 5 U.S. 137 (1803)
2. Maltz, *Politics of Slavery*, 63
3. Ibid.
4. Ibid.
5. Franklin, *Slavery to Freedom*, 65
6. Ibid, 67
7. Ibid, 94
8. Ibid, 95
9. Stampp, *Peculiar Institution*, 26
10. Earl M. Maltz. *Slavery and the Supreme Court, 1825-1861*. (Lawrence: University of Kansas Press, 2009), 222.
11. Franklin, *Slavery to Freedom*, 214-215
12. Ibid.
13. Ibid, 215-216
14. Ibid, 214
15. Ibid, 216
16. Allen, *Origins of the Dred Scott case*, 141-142 (from December 1, 1833 until May 29, 1840)
17. Maltz, *Politics of Slavery*, 67.
18. Ibid, 67
19. Ibid.
20. Ibid, 67-68
21. Ibid, 67-68
22. Ibid, 70-71
23. Strader v. Graham, 51 U.S. 82 (1851)
24. Maltz, *Politics of Slavery*, 70
25. Allen, *Origins of the Dred Scott case*, 48-149
26. Maltz, *Politics of Slavery*, 72
27. Ibid, 75

28   Allen, *Origins of the Dred Scott case*, 149
29   Maltz, *Politics of Slavery*, 105
30   Allen, *Origins of the Dred Scott case*, 160
31   Maltz, *Politics of Slavery*, 131
32   Allen, *Origins of the Dred Scott case*, 167
33   Maltz, *Politics of Slavery*. 118-123; *Dred Scott*, 60 U.S. at 407. Chief Justice Roger B. Taney writing the Opinion of the Court stated,"[t]hey [Africans, the race to whom the Scotts belonged] had for more than a century before been regarded as beings of an inferior order, and altogether unfit to associate with the white race, either in social or political relations;…"
34   Maltz, *Politics of Slavery*, 118.

Notes to Chapter 3: The Legacy Of Dred Scott

1   Maltz, *Politics of Slavery*, 140
2   Ibid.
3   Phillip Shaw Paludan. *The Presidency of Abraham Lincoln*, (Lawrence: University of Kansas Press, 1994), 5.
4   Maltz, *Slavery and the Supreme Court*, 290.
5   Ibid, 274-275.
6   Ibid, 273.
7   Ibid, 273.
8   Paludan, *The Presidency*, 6.
9   Korematsu v. United States, 323 U.S. 214 (1944).
10   Stephen Breyer, *Making Our Democracy Work A Judge's View*. (New York: Alfred A. Knopf, a division of Random House, 2010) 42.
11   Maltz, *Slavery and the Supreme Court*, 266-267.
12   *Dred Scott*, 60 U.S. at 454.
13   Maltz, *Slavery and the Supreme Court*, 269.
14   Ibid, 301.

15 Ibid, 268.
16 Paludan, *The Presidency*, 299
17 U.S. Const. amend. XIV
18 William B. Glidden, *Congress and the Fourteenth Amendment: enforcing liberty and equality in the states.* (Plymouth, United Kingdom: Lexington Books, 2013), 36.
19 Civil Rights Cases, 109 U.S. 3 (1883).
20 Heart of Atlanta Motel, Inc. v. United States, 379 U.S. 241 (1964)
21 Ibid.
22 Shelby County v. Holder, 570 U.S. 529 (2013)
23 Voting Rights Act, 52 U.S.C §10304(a) (1965).
24 Breyer, *Making our Democracy*, 44.
25 Ibid, 43
26 Dr. Martin Luther King, J. ,*Where do we go From Here: Chaos or Community,* (Boston: Beacon Press, 1968), 18.
27 Ethan Greenberg, *Dred Scott and the Dangers of a Political Court,* (Lanham: Lexington Books, 2009), 201.

Notes to Chapter 4: The Activist: Homer Plessy

1 Jeffrey Rosen, *The Supreme Court: The Personalities and Rivalries that Defined America,* (New York: Times Books Henry Holt Company,2006), 94.
2 Medley, Keith, W., *We as Freeman, Plessy v. Ferguson: The Fight Against Legal Segregation*,(Louisiana: Pelican Publishing Company, Inc., (2003), 20.
3 "PLESSY, Homer Adolph," Dictionary of Louisiana Biography, Louisiana Historical Association, December 23, 2018, https://www.lahistory.org/resources/dictionary-louisiana-biography/dictionary-louisiana-biography-p/.
4 .Medley, *We as Freeman*, 14.
5 Ibid, 24

6   Ibid, 25

7   Rosen, *The Supreme Court*, 94.

8   Medley, *We as Freeman*, 21.

9   Jules Lobel, *Success Without Victory: Lost Legal Battles and the Long Road to Justice in America*, (New York: New York University Press, 2003),104.

10   Ibid.

11   Dr. Martin Luther King, Jr., "Letter From A Birmingham Jail," The Martin Luther King, Jr., Research and Education Institute, Stanford University, Apri 27, 2020, https://kinginstitute.stanford.edu/king-papers/documents/letter-birmingham-jail.

12   Harvey Fireside, *Separate and Unequal/Homer Plessy and the Supreme Court Decision that Legalized Racism*, (New York: Caroll & Graf Publishers, an Imprint of Avalon Publishing, 2004), 3.

13   Ibid.

14   Lobel, *Success Without Victory*,100

15   Ibid, 101

16   Ibid, 101

Notes to Chapter 5: A Case of Conscience: *Plessy V. Ferguson*

1   Rosen, *The Supreme Court*, 94

2   Ibid.

3   Ibid, 95

4   Ibid.

5   Ibid.

6   Ibid.

7   Ibid, 96

8   Lobel, *Success Without Victory*, 109-110

9   Gordon Andrews, *Undoing Plessy: Charles Hamilton Houston, Race, Labor, and the Law, 1895-1950*, (Newcastle: Cambridge Scholars Publishing, 2014), 21-22.
10 Ibid.
11 Ibid.
12 Ibid.
13 Lobel, *Success Without Victory*, 105-106
14 Ibid.
15 Ibid.
16 Lobel, *Success Without Victory*, 108-109
17 Lobel, *Success Without Victory*, 110
18 Lawrence Goldstone, *Inherently Unequal: The Betrayal of Equal Rights by the Supreme Court 1865-1903*. (New York: Walker Publishing Company, 2011), 164.
19 *Landmark Cases, Historic Supreme Court Decisions*, season 2 episode 4. "Plessy v. Ferguson," featuring Theodore Shaw and Michael Klarman, aired March 19, 2018, https://www.c-span.org/video/?440867-1/supreme-court-landmark-case-plessy-v-ferguson (These Justices were, Edward D. White, Rufus Peckham, David Brewer, who did not participate in the *Plessy* case, George Shiras, Stephen J. Field, and Horace Gray).
20 Andrews, *Undoing Plessy*, 44.
21 Andrews, *Undoing Plessy*, 18-19
22 Ibid.
23 Ibid.
24 Ibid, 19
25 Ibid, 19-20
26 Andrews, *Undoing Plessy*, 44
27 Andrews, *Undoing Plessy*, 44
28 Lobel, *Success Without Victory*, 110-111
29 Lobel, *Success Without Victory*, 111-112

30 Lobel, *Success Without Victory*, 112-113
31 Ibid.
32 Ibid.
33 Goldstone, *Inherently Unequal*, 163
34 Ibid.
35 Melvin I. Urofsky, *The Public Debate over Controversia Supreme Court Decisions* . (Washington D.C. : CQ Press, a division of Congressional Quarterly, Inc., 2006), 75.
36 Ibid.
37 Lobel, *Success Without Victory*, 113
38 Andrews, *Undoing Plessy*, 45-46
39 Ibid.
40 Ibid.
41 Ibid.
42 Lobel, *Success Without Victory*, 113
43 Ibid.

Notes to Chapter 6: Fail Up: The Outcomes Of Plessy

1 Lobel, *Success Without Victory*, 114-115
2 Ibid; Urofsky, *The Public Debate*, 76
3 Goldstone, *Inherently Unequal*, 168
4 Ibid.
5 Urofsky, *The Public Debate*, 77
6 Ibid.
7 Ibid, 76
8 Ibid, 77
9 Goldstone, *Inherently Unequal*, 168
10 Ibid.
11 Urofsky, *The Public Debate*, 79
12 Ibid, 77.

13 Ibid.
14 Ibid.
15 Ibid, 79.
16 Ibid.
17 Mark M. Smith, *How Race is Made: Slavery, Segregation, and the Senses*, (The University of North Carolina Press, 2008), 74.
18 Ibid, 75
19 Ibid.
20 Goldstone, *Inherently Unequal*, 186.
21 Ibid,167.
22 Andrews, *Undoing Plessy*, 50.
23 Smith, *How Race is Made*, 75
24 Ibid, 77
25 Harvey Fireside, *Separate and Unequal/Homer Plessy and the Supreme Court Decision that Legalized Racism* (New York: Caroll & Graf Publishers, an Imprint of Avalon Publishing, 2004), 1.
26 "NCCU Law School History," September 24, 2019, http://law.nccu.edu/about/history/.
27 Rosen, *The Supreme Court*, 100
28 Urofsky, *The Public Debate*, 82
29 Rosen, *The Supreme Court*, 100
30 Lobel, *Success Without Victory*, 122-124
31 Urofsky, *The Public Debate*, 76
32 Fireside, *Separate and Unequal*, 162
33 Goldstone, *Inherently Unequal*, 169-170
34 Ibid.
35 Ibid, 170
36 Ibid.
37 Lobel, *Success Without Victory*, 121-122
38 Ibid.
39 Urofsky, *The Public Debate*, 76

40 Ibid, 80-81
41 Ibid, 81-82
42 Lobel, *Success Without Victory*, 118-119

Notes to Chapter 7: An Education: The Road To Brown V. Board Of Education

1   Clare Cushman and Melvin I. Urofsky, *Black White and Brown, Black, White, and Brown: The Landmark School Desegregation Case in Retrospect*, (Washington D.C. : CQ Press, a division of Congressional Quarterly, Inc., 2004), 151-154.
2   Ibid, 152
3   Ibid, 152
4   Michael J. Klarman, *From Jim Crow to Civil Rights*. (New York: Oxford University Press, 2004), 25.
5   Ibid.
6   Ibid.
7   Cushman and Urofsky, *Black White and Brown*, 292.
8   Dr. Martin Luther King, Jr., "Letter From A Birmingham Jail," The Martin Luther King, Jr., Research and Education Institute, Stanford University, Apri 27, 2020, https://kinginstitute.stanford.edu/king-papers/documents/letter-birmingham-jail.
9   Ibid, 69-70.

Notes to Chapter 8: Reaching The Mountain Top

1   Richard Kluger, *Simple Justice: The History of Brown v. Board of Education and Black America's Struggle for Equality*, (New York: First Vintage Books a Division of Random House, 2004), 281.
2   Sipuel v. the University of Oklahoma, 332 U.S. 631 (1948).
3   Murray v. Pearson, 169 Md. 478, 182 A. 590 (1936)
4   Kluger, *Simple Justice*, 294-295

5   Ibid, 301
6   Davis v. County School Board of Prince Edward County, 103 F. Supp. 337 (1952).
7   Gebhart v. Belton, 87 A.2d 862 (Del. Ch. 1952) *aff'd*, 91 A.2d 137 (Del. 1952)
8   Bolling v. Sharpe, 347 U.S. 497 (1954)
9   Kluger, *Simple Justice*, 302
10 Ibid.
11 Juan Wiliams, *Thurgood Marshall American Revolutionary*, (New York: Times Books, a Divion of Random House, Inc., 1998), 204.
12 Kluger, *Simple Justice*, 195
13 *Brown, et al. v. Board of Education of Topeka, Kansas, et al.* 349 U.S. 294, 301(1955)
14 Wiliams, *Thurgood Marshall*, 219
15 Paul B. Sheatsley, *White Attitudes Toward the Negro*, (Boston: American Academy of Arts and Science, 1966), 219.
16 Cushman and Urofsky, *Black White and Brown*, 21.
17 Ibid, 19.
18 Ibid, 2
19 Ibid.
20 Ibid, 172.
21 Gebhart v. Belton, 91 A.2d 137, (Del. 1952)
22 Brown v. Board of Education of Topeka Kansas, 347 U.S. 483, 495 (1954)
23 Klarman, *From Jim Crow*, 416.
24 Cushman and Urofsky, *Black White and Brown*, 28
25 Ibid, 153.

Notes to Chapter 9: The Struggle Continues

1   Urofsky, *The Public Debate*, 29

2   Ibid; Lockner v. New York, 198 U.S 45 (1905) (In *Lochner*, the Court held that working time limits violated the 14th Amendment, and considered statistics regarding the health of trades and occupations to compare with that of bakers, which was the trade involved in the case); Adair v. U.S., 208 U.S. 161, (1908) (In *Adair*, the Court held that prohibitions on workers joining unions were unconstitutional); Adkins v. Children's Hospital, 261 U.S. 525 (1923) (In *Adkins*, the Court held that minimum wage federal laws for women were unconstitutional).

3   Urofsky, *The Public Debate*, 29
4   Urofsky, *The Public Debate*, 175
5   Brown v. Board of Education of Topeka, 349 U.S. 294 (1955).
6   Urofsky, *The Public Debate*, 181
7   Brown, 349 US at 307.
8   Urofsky, *The Public Debate*, 182.
9   Urofsky, *The Public Debate*, 196
10 Urofsky, *The Public Debate*, 153
11 Urofsky, *The Public Debate*, 154.
12 Jennifer L. Hochschild and Nathan B. Scovronick, *The American Dream and the Public Schools*, (New York: Oxford University Press, 2003), 32
13 James T. Patterson, *Grand Expectations: The United States, 1945-1974*, (New York: Oxford University Press, 1996), 389
14 Urofsky, *The Public Debate*, 416
15 Ibid.
16 Ibid, 417
17 Ibid, 27
18 Ibid, 197
19 Ibid.
20 Ibid.
21 Ibid, 154.

22   Ibid, 154-155

23   Mapp v. Ohio, 367 U.S. 643 (1961) (In *Mapp*, the Court held that states cannot use illegally seized evidence against criminal defendants); Gideon v. Wainwright, 372 U.S. 335 (1963) (In *Gideon*, the Court held that criminal defendants that cannot afford a lawyer mut be provided a one for their defense); Miranda v. Arizona, 384 U.S. 436 (1966) (In *Miranda*, the Court held that statements made by criminal defendants during interrogation when in custody, may not be used against them, unless they were first informed of their right not to incriminate themselves and their right to a lawyer).

24   Swann v. Mecklenberg County Board of Education, 402 U.S. 1 (1971) (In *Swann*, the Supreme Court ruled that forced busing was an appropriate remedy to accomplish the goal of school integration.)

25   City of Richmond v. J.A. Croson, 488 U.S. 469 (1989) (In *Croson*, the Supreme Court held that set-aside contracts for minority contractors was unconstitutional.); Adarand Constructors, Inc. v. Pena, 515 U.S. 200 (1995) (In *Adarand*, the Supreme Court held that racial classifications imposed by the federal government are held to strict scrutiny review, which is the highest review possible, and requires that the law must be narrowly tailored to meet a compelling governmental interest); Grutter v. Bollinger, 539 U.S. 306 (2003) (In *Grutter*, the Supreme Court upheld the affirmative action program of the University of Michigan Law School, based on its individualized consideration of applicants.); Gratz v. Bollinger, 539 U.S. 244 (2003)(In *Gratz*, the Supreme Court struck down the affirmative action undergraduate admissions program for the University of Michigan as unconstitutional).

Notes to Chapter 10: Lessons From Movement Mentors

1. U.S. Congress, House, *Emmett Till Antilynching Act*, HR 35, 116th Cong., introduced in House January 3, 2019, https://www.congress.gov/bill/116th-congress/house-bill/35. ("At least 4,742 people, predominantly African Americans, were reported lynched in the United States between 1882 and 1968").

2. *Dred Scott*, 60 U.S at 405 (In his majority opinion in *Dred Scott*, Chief Justice Taney indicated that it was the inaction and ineffectiveness of the other two branches of the federal government which precipitated the Court's reluctant entrance into the issue of slavery and the U.S. Constitution.

3. Linda Brown and her sister founded the Brown Foundation for Educational Equity. https://brownvboard.org.

4. Derrick A. Bell, "Brown v. Board of Education and the Interest-Convergence Dilemma." *Harvard Law Review 93*, no, 3 (1980): 524.

5. Wiliams, *Thurgood Marshall*, 220

6. Rawn James, Jr., *Root and Branch: Charles Hamilton Houston, Thurgood Marshall, and the Struggled to End Segregation*, (New York: Bloomsbury Press, 2010), 221.

7. King, J., *Where do we go*, 18.

8. Gayle v. Browder, 352 U.S. 903 (1956), affirming Browder v. Gayle, 142 F. Supp. 707 (1956 (In *Browder*, a three-judge panel of the U.S. District Court for the Middle District of Alabama, by a vote of 2-1 ruled that segregation in busing is unconstitutional in violation of the Equal Protection Clause of the 14th Amendment to the U.S. Constitution).

www.ingramcontent.com/pod-product-compliance
Lightning Source LLC
Chambersburg PA
CBHW051428290426
44109CB00016B/1471